D1231506

SKETCHES AND REVIEWS

SKETCHES AND REVIEWS
BY WALTER PATER

Essay Index Reprint Series

BOOKS FOR LIBRARIES PRESS
FREEPORT, NEW YORK

First Published 1919
Reprinted 1969

STANDARD BOOK NUMBER:
8369-1371-X

LIBRARY OF CONGRESS CATALOG CARD NUMBER:
77-99718

PRINTED IN THE UNITED STATES OF AMERICA

LIBRARY
FLORIDA S TF UNIVERSITY
TALLAHASSEE, FLORIDA

FOREWORD

This volume is the first collection in book form of nearly all the known fugitive writings of Walter Pater, since the posthumously published "Essays from the Guardian" appeared nearly a quarter of a century ago. A reviewer in the *Athenæum* furnished a complete list of all the uncollected articles and reviews by Pater, when noticing the "Guardian" essays. It is scarcely necessary to state that Pater polished his book reviews with the same elaborate care that he did his other essays.

Some of the authors reviewed by Pater have attained in our time an almost cosmopolitan fame. Indeed the names of writers like Fabre, Symonds, George Moore, Arthur Symons and Oscar Wilde are to-day as well known as that of Pater himself. These men no doubt realized they were very fortunate in having so distinguished and scrupulous a reviewer. George Moore tells in his *Avowals,*

published in the *Pall Mall Magazine* (in
America in *Lippincott's Magazine*), of the
great thrill he experienced in reading the review of his *Modern Painting* by "the greatest
writer in the world." He even complains that
C. L. Shadwell did not mention this review in
his incomplete bibliography of Pater, published
in the volume of miscellaneous essays by Pater.
Oscar Wilde was especially happy that his *Picture of Dorian Gray* should have been the subject of an essay from the pen of his master.
Arthur Symons, then a rising poet, owes, no
doubt, part of his early fame to Pater's review.
The two essays on Flaubert give us an insight
into the English critic's own indebtedness to
the supreme French stylist.

The essays and reviews in this volume appeared in the *Athenæum*, the *Bookman* (London), *Macmillan's Magazine*, the *Pall Mall
Gazette*, the London *Daily Chronicle* and the
Westminster Review.

ALBERT MORDELL.

Philadelphia,
March, 1919.

CONTENTS

SKETCHES AND REVIEWS

ÆSTHETIC POETRY

THE "æsthetic" poetry is neither a mere reproduction of Greek or mediæval poetry, nor only an idealisation of modern life and sentiment. The atmosphere on which its effect depends belongs to no simple form of poetry, no actual form of life. Greek poetry, mediæval or modern poetry, projects, above the realities of its time, a world in which the forms of things are transfigured. Of that transfigured world this new poetry takes possession, and sublimates beyond it another still fainter and more spectral, which is literally an artificial or "earthly paradise." It is a finer ideal, extracted from what in relation to any actual world is already an ideal. Like some strange second flowering after date, it renews on a more delicate type the poetry of a past age, but must not be confounded with it. The secret of the enjoyment

1

of it is that inversion of homesickness known to some, that incurable thirst for the sense of escape, which no actual form of life satisfies, no poetry even, if it be merely simple and spontaneous.

The writings of the "romantic school," of which the æsthetic poetry is an afterthought, mark a transition not so much from the pagan to the mediæval ideal, as from a lower to a higher degree of passion in literature. The end of the eighteenth century, swept by vast disturbing currents, experienced an excitement of spirit of which one note was a reaction against an outworn classicism severed not more from nature than from the genuine motives of ancient art; and a return to true Hellenism was as much a part of this reaction as the sudden preoccupation with things mediæval. The mediæval tendency is in Goethe's *Goetz von Berlichingen,* the Hellenic in his *Iphigenie.* At first this mediævalism was superficial, or at least external. Adventure, romance in the frankest sense, grotesque individualism—that is one element in mediæval poetry, and with it alone Scott and Goethe dealt. Beyond them were the two other elements of the mediæval spirit: its mystic religion at its apex in Dante and Saint Louis, and its mystic passion, passing here and there into the great romantic loves of rebellious flesh, of Lancelot and Abelard. That stricter, imaginative mediævalism which re-creates the mind of the Middle Age, so that the form, the presentment grows outward from within, came later with Victor Hugo in France, with Heine in Germany.

In the *Defence of Guenevere: and Other Poems,* published by Mr. William Morris now many years ago, the first typical specimen of æsthetic poetry, we have a refinement upon this later, profounder mediævalism. The poem which gives its name to the volume is a thing tormented and awry with passion, like the body of Guenevere defending herself from the charge of adultery, and the accent falls in strange, unwonted places with the effect of a great cry. In truth these Arthurian legends,

in their origin prior to Christianity, yield all
their sweetness only in a Christian atmosphere.
What is characteristic in them is the strange
suggestion of a deliberate choice between
Christ and a rival lover. That religion, monastic religion at any rate, has its sensuous side,
a dangerously sensuous side, has been often
seen: it is the experience of Rousseau as well as
of the Christian mystics. The Christianity of
the Middle Age made way among a people
whose loss was in the life of the senses, partly
by its æsthetic beauty, a thing so profoundly
felt by the Latin hymn-writers, who for one
moral or spiritual sentiment have a hundred
sensuous images. And so in those imaginative
loves, in their highest expression, the Provençal poetry, it is a rival religion with a new rival
cultus that we see. Coloured through and
through with Christian sentiment, they are
rebels against it. The rejection of one worship
for another is never lost sight of. The jealousy of that other lover, for whom these words
and images and refined ways of sentiment were

first devised, is the secret here of a borrowed, perhaps factitious colour and heat. It is the mood of the cloister taking a new direction, and winning so a later space of life it never anticipated.

Hereon, as before in the cloister, so now in the *château,* the reign of reverie set in. The devotion of the cloister knew that mood thoroughly, and had sounded all its stops. For the object of this devotion was absent or veiled, not limited to one supreme plastic form like Zeus at Olympia or Athena in the Acropolis, but distracted, as in a fever dream, into a thousand symbols and reflections. But then, the Church, that new Sibyl, had a thousand secrets to make the absent near. Into this kingdom of reverie, and with it into a paradise of ambitious refinements, the earthly love enters, and becomes a prolonged somnambulism. Of religion it learns the art of directing towards an unseen object sentiments whose natural direction is towards objects of sense. Hence a love defined by the absence of the beloved, choosing to be without hope, protesting against all lower uses of love, barren, extravagant, antinomian. It is the love which is incompatible with marriage, for the chevalier who never comes, of the serf for the *châtelaine,* of the rose for the nightingale, of Rudel for the Lady of Tripoli. Another element of extravagance came in with the feudal spirit: Provençal love is full of the very forms of vassalage. To be the servant of love, to have offended, to taste the subtle luxury of chastisement, of reconciliation—the religious spirit, too, knows that, and meets just there, as in Rousseau, the delicacies of the earthly love. Here, under this strange complex of conditions, as in some medicated air, exotic flowers of sentiment expand, among people of a remote and unaccustomed beauty, somnambulistic, frail, androgynous, the light almost shining through them. Surely, such loves were too fragile and adventurous to last more than for a moment.

That monastic religion of the Middle Age was, in fact, in many of its bearings, like a beautiful disease or disorder of the senses: and a religion which is a disorder of the senses must always be subject to illusions. Reverie, illusion, delirium: they are the three stages of a fatal descent both in the religion and the loves of the Middle Age. Nowhere has the impression of this delirium been conveyed as by Victor Hugo in *Notre Dame de Paris.* The strangest creations of sleep seem here, by some appalling licence, to cross the limit of the dawn. The English poet too has learned the secret. He has diffused through *King Arthur's Tomb* the maddening white glare of the sun, and tyranny of the moon, not tender and far-off, but close down—the sorcerer's moon, large and feverish. The colouring is intricate and delirious, as of "scarlet lilies." The influence of summer is like a poison in one's blood, with a sudden bewildered sickening of life and all things. In *Galahad: a Mystery,* the frost of Christmas night on the chapel stones acts as a strong narcotic: a sudden shrill ringing pierces through the numbness: a voice proclaims that the Grail has gone forth through the great forest. It is in the *Blue Closet* that this delirium reaches its height with a singular beauty, reserved perhaps for the enjoyment of the few.

A passion of which the outlets are sealed, begets a tension of nerve, in which the sensible world comes to one with a reinforced brilliancy and relief—all redness is turned into blood, all water into tears. Hence a wild, convulsed sensuousness in the poetry of the Middle Age, in which the things of nature begin to play a strange delirious part. Of the things of nature the mediæval mind had a deep sense; but its sense of them was not objective, no real escape to the world without us. The aspects and motions of nature only reinforced its prevailing mood, and were in conspiracy with one's own brain against one. A single sentiment invaded the world: everything was infused with a motive drawn from the soul. The amorous poetry of Provence, making the starling and the swallow its messengers, illustrates the whole attitude of nature in this electric atmosphere, bent as by miracle or magic to the service of human passion.

The most popular and gracious form of Provençal poetry was the *nocturn,* sung by the lover at night at the door or under the window of his mistress. These songs were of different kinds, according to the hour at which they were intended to be sung. Some were to be sung at midnight—songs inviting to sleep, the *serena,* or *serenade;* others at break of day— waking songs, the *aube* or *aubade.*[1] This waking-song is put sometimes into the mouth of a comrade of the lover, who plays sentinel during the night, to watch for and announce the dawn: sometimes into the mouth of one of the lovers, who are about to separate. A modification of it is familiar to us all in *Romeo and Juliet,* where the lovers debate whether the song they hear is of the nightingale or the lark; the au-bade, with the two other great forms of love-

---

[1] Fauriel's *Histoire de la Poésie Provencale,* tome ii. ch. xviii.

poetry then floating in the world, the sonnet and the epithalamium, being here refined, heightened, and inwoven into the structure of the play. Those, in whom what Rousseau calls *les frayeurs nocturnes* are constitutional, know what splendour they give to the things of the morning; and how there comes something of relief from physical pain with the first white film in the sky. The Middle Age knew those terrors in all their forms; and these songs of the morning win hence a strange tenderness and effect. The crown of the English poet's book is one of these appreciations of the dawn:—

"Pray but one prayer for me 'twixt thy closed lips,
    Think but one thought of me up in the stars.
The summer-night waneth, the morning light slips,
    Faint and gray 'twixt the leaves of the aspen,
        betwixt the cloud-bars,
That are patiently waiting there for the dawn:
    Patient and colourless, though Heaven's gold
Waits to float through them along with the sun.
Far out in the meadows, above the young corn,
    The heavy elms wait, and restless and cold
The uneasy wind rises; the roses are dun;

Through the long twilight they pray for the dawn,
Round the lone house in the midst of the corn.
  Speak but one word to me over the corn,
  Over the tender, bow'd locks of the corn."

It is the very soul of the bridegroom which goes forth to the bride: inanimate things are longing with him: all the sweetness of the imaginative loves of the Middle Age, with a superadded spirituality of touch all its own, is in that!

The *Defence of Guenevere* was published in 1858; the *Life and Death of Jason* in 1867; to be followed by *The Earthly Paradise;* and the change of manner wrought in the interval, entire, almost a revolt, is characteristic of the æsthetic poetry. Here there is no delirium or illusion, no experiences of mere soul while the body and the bodily senses sleep, or wake with convulsed intensity at the prompting of imaginative love; but rather the great primary passions under broad daylight as of the pagan Veronese. This simplification interests us, not merely for the sake of an individual poet—full of charm as he is—but chiefly because it explains through him a transition which, under many forms, is one law of the life of the human spirit, and of which what we call the Renaissance is only a supreme instance. Just so the monk in his cloister, through the "open vision," open only to the spirit, divined, aspired to, and at last apprehended, a better daylight, but earthly, open only to the senses. Complex and subtle interests, which the mind spins for itself, may occupy art and poetry or our own spirits for a time; but sooner or later they come back with a sharp rebound to the simple elementary passions—anger, desire, regret, pity, and fear: and what corresponds to them in the sensuous world—bare, abstract fire, water, air, tears, sleep, silence, and what De Quincey has called the "glory of motion."

This reaction from dreamlight to daylight gives, as always happens, a strange power in dealing with morning and the things of the morning. Not less is this Hellenist of the

Middle Age master of dreams, of sleep and the desire of sleep—sleep in which no one walks, restorer of childhood to men—dreams, not like Galahad's or Guenevere's, but full of happy, childish wonder as in the earlier world. It is a world in which the centaur and the ram with the fleece of gold are conceivable. The song sung always claims to be sung for the first time. There are hints at a language common to birds and beasts and men. Everywhere there is an impression of surprise, as of people first waking from the golden age, at fire, snow, wine, the touch of water as one swims, the salt taste of the sea. And this simplicity at first hand is a strange contrast to the sought-out simplicity of Wordsworth. Desire here is towards the body of nature for its own sake, not because a soul is divined through it.

And yet it is one of the charming anachronisms of a poet, who, while he handles an ancient subject, never becomes an antiquarian, but animates his subject by keeping it always close to himself, that between whiles we have a sense of English scenery as from an eye well practised under Wordsworth's influence, as from "the casement half opened on summer-nights," with the song of the brown bird among the willows, the

"Noise of bells, such as in moonlit lanes
Rings from the grey team on the market night."

Nowhere but in England is there such a "paradise of birds," the fern-owl, the water-hen, the thrush in a hundred sweet variations, the gerfalcon, the kestrel, the starling, the pea-fowl; birds heard from the field by the townsman down in the streets at dawn; doves everywhere, pink-footed, grey-winged, flitting about the temple, troubled by the temple incense, trapped in the snow. The sea-touches are not less sharp and firm, surest of effect in places where river and sea, salt and fresh waves, conflict.

In handling a subject of Greek legend, anything in the way of an actual revival must always be impossible. Such vain antiquarianism is a waste of the poet's power. The composite experience of all the ages is part of each one of us; to deduct from that experience, to obliterate any part of it, to come face to face with the people of a past age, as if the Middle Age, the Renaissance, the eighteenth century had not been, is as impossible as to become a little child, or enter again into the womb and be born. But though it is not possible to repress a single phase of that humanity, which, because we live and move and have our being in the life of humanity, makes us what we are, it is possible to isolate such a phase, to throw it into relief, to be divided against ourselves in zeal for it; as we may hark back to some choice space of our own individual life. We cannot truly conceive the age: we can conceive the element it has contributed to our culture: we can treat the subjects of the age bringing that into relief. Such an attitude towards Greece, aspiring to but never actually reaching its way of conceiving life, is what is possible for art.

The modern poet or artist who treats in this

way a classical story comes very near, if not to
the Hellenism of Homer, yet to the Hellenism
of Chaucer, the Hellenism of the Middle Age,
or rather of that exquisite first period of the
Renaissance within it.   Afterwards the Renaissance takes its side, becomes, perhaps, exaggerated or facile.   But the choice life of the
human spirit is always under mixed lights, and
in mixed situations, when it is not too sure of
itself, is still expectant, girt up to leap forward
to the promise.   Such a situation there was in
that earliest return from the overwrought spiritualities of the Middle Age to the earlier, more
ancient life of the senses; and for us the most
attractive form of classical story is the monk's
conception of it, when he escapes from the
sombre atmosphere of his cloister to natural
light.   The fruits of this mood, which, divining
more than it understands, infuses into the
scenery and figures of Christian history some
subtle reminiscence of older gods, or into the
story of Cupid and Psyche that passionate
stress of spirit which the world owes to Chris-

tianity, constitute a peculiar vein of interest in the art of the fifteenth century.

And so, before we leave *Jason* and *The Earthly Paradise,* a word must be said about their mediævalisms, delicate inconsistencies, which, coming in a poem of Greek subject, bring into this white dawn thoughts of the delirious night just over and make one's sense of relief deeper. The opening of the fourth book of *Jason* describes the embarkation of the Argonauts: as in a dream, the scene shifts and we go down from Iolchos to the sea through a pageant of the Middle Age in some French or Italian town. The gilded vanes on the spires, the bells ringing in the towers, the trellis of roses at the window, the close planted with apple-trees, the grotesque undercroft with its close-set pillars, change by a single touch the air of these Greek cities and we are at Glastonbury by the tomb of Arthur. The nymph in furred raiment who seduces Hylas is conceived frankly in the spirit of Teutonic romance; her song is of a garden enclosed, such as that with

which the old church glass-stainer surrounds
the mystic bride of the song of songs. Medea
herself has a hundred touches of the mediæval
sorceress, the sorceress of the Streckelberg or
the Blocksberg: her mystic changes are Christ-
abel's. It is precisely this effect, this grace of
Hellenism relieved against the sorrow of the
Middle Age, which forms the chief motives of
The Earthly Paradise: with an exquisite dex-
terity the two threads of sentiment are here
interwoven and contrasted. A band of adven-
turers sets out from Norway, most northerly of
northern lands, where the plague is raging—
the bell continually ringing as they carry the
Sacrament to the sick. Even in Mr. Morris's
earliest poems snatches of the sweet French
tongue had always come with something of
Hellenic blitheness and grace. And now it is
below the very coast of France, through the
fleet of Edward the Third, among the gaily
painted mediæval sails, that we pass to a reserved fragment of Greece, which by some divine good fortune lingers on in the western sea

into the Middle Age. There the stories of *The Earthly Paradise* are told, Greek story and romantic alternating; and for the crew of the *Rose Garland,* coming across the sins of the earlier world with the sign of the cross, and drinking Rhine-wine in Greece, the two worlds of sentiment are confronted.

One characteristic of the pagan spirit the æsthetic poetry has, which is on its surface— the continual suggestion, pensive or passionate,. of the shortness of life. This is contrasted with the bloom of the world, and gives new seduction to it—the sense of death and the desire of beauty: the desire of beauty quickened by the sense of death. But that complexion of sentiment is at its height in another "æsthetic" poet of whom I have to speak next, Dante Gabriel Rossetti.

M. LEMAITRE'S "SERENUS, AND OTHER TALES"

A VOLUME of fiction which, while it possesses something of the power and charm of Gustave Flaubert, takes us through no scenes of cruelty or coarseness, but relies for its interest on the blameless pathos of life, touched in the spirit of a true realism, is worth pointing out to English readers. The volume takes its name from the singular story of Serenus, a Christian martyr, to which are added certain briefer *Stories Of The Past And Of To-day*. With two slight exceptions, two pieces of peculiarly Parisian humour, which make a harsh contrast with the rest of the book, these stories are as pure and solemn as the pictures of Alphonse Legros. The narrative of Serenus, the patrician martyr, has about it something which reminds one of those sumptuous Roman basilicas put together out of the marble fragments of older pagan temples or palaces; and in the shorter pieces the busy French journalist seems to have gone for a sort of mental holiday to quiet convent parlours and white-washed village churches—places of subdued colour and personages congruous therewith, pleasant, doubtless, to fatigued Parisian eyes. M. Jules Lemaitre is before all things an artist, showing in these pieces, the longest of which attains no more than sixty pages, that self-possession and sustained sense of design which anticipates the end in the commencement, and never loses sight of it—that gift of literary structure which lends so monumental an air to even the shortest of Flaubert's pieces. Then, he has Flaubert's sense of compassion and his peculiar interest in certain phases or aspects of religious life; and his art (again like Flaubert's) is a learned art. There is the fruit of much and varied reading and thought in this volume, short as it is, though without a shade of pedantry; and its union of realism, of the force of style which is allied to a genuine realism, with an entire freedom from the dubious interests of almost all French fiction, gives it a charming freshness of effect.

We propose to say a few words on those shorter pieces first, giving some specimens of M. Lemaitre's manner. The hero of *La Mère Sainte-Agathe,* a very intellectual young Parisian, has formed a somewhat artificial marriage engagement with a guileless orphan-girl at the convent school over which Mother Sainte-Agathe presides. Mother Sainte-Agathe was still young—thirty years, perhaps thirty-five. But years, in the case of "the religious," when they are pretty and live really holy lives, rather embalm them than add to their age. When the young man visits the girl, the Mother presides over their interviews, looking at them with an air of kindness and serenity, with an expression she wore always, in which one seemed to detect the presence of a thought, unique, eternal in its character, ever mingled with the thought of the

present hour.   One day the girl leads her lover
into the convent garden.

"It was a large one, and so neat and prim!—neat
and prim as a convent-chapel.   An avenue of limes,
as exact in line as a row of tapers, led to a terrace
projecting on the Loire, with a pleasing view over
the landscape of Touraine.   Between its gentle
banks, amid scattered groups of rustling poplars,
the river spread out like a lake, with little pale-
coloured islands tufted with misty beds of osiers, and
against the horizon a long, long bridge of delicate
arches, silver-grey—all very sweet, with melting out-
lines in water colour tints, under a lightsome sky of
soft blue."

But the childish lover is shrewd enough to
notice that in these visits the real business of
conversation (very superior conversation, on
M. Renan, for instance) is wholly between the
Mother and the clever young man.   She writes
one day at the end of one of her letters:
"Mother Sainte-Agathe tells me that I don't
put warmth enough into my letters.   Ah! my
friend, I have enough of it in my heart nevertheless; only perhaps I am still too little to

know how to tell it." The young man does not marry the orphan, and, of course, not the reverend Mother. He thought it well to discontinue his visits to the convent.

"Almost without note of the fact," he says, "I was treating Lydia like a child. Whenever I said anything at all serious it was to Mother Sainte Agathe I addressed myself.

"They were exquisite, those conversations with the Mother—all the more exquisite because I was then finishing a volume of criticism and fantasy combined, in which I put the utmost amount of Renanism, Impressionism, and Parisian raillery, in turn or altogether. And it was often after the reading of some perverse book that I took myself to those white interviews. One day at parting, when I kissed Lydia, I saw tears in her eyes. 'You are crying, Lydia: have I hurt you in any way?' She gave me a long, serious look, and the look was no longer that of a mere child. 'Are you quite sure,' she said to me in a low voice, 'that it is still for my sake that you come here?'

"It haunted me through the evening, through the whole night, little Lydia's question. In spite of myself she had revealed to me what was at the bottom of my heart. In effect, I perceived with much distress that for some time past it was for Mother Sainte-

Agathe I had come, that that charm of innocence in my betrothed was exhausted. Yes, it was over—well over!

"I did not venture to the convent next day, nor the day after that. Did she look out for me? I never returned there again."

A still more melancholy note is struck in *L'Ainée,* the story of a beautiful girl, the eldest of eight sisters, who sees them all cheerfully married to the suitors who had begun by paying court to herself. It pained her to see her nephews and nieces, although she loved them much, and spent her days in work for them. And what added to her unhappiness was that every one, in these matters, took her for a *confidante* and adviser, regarding her as a person of extraordinary prudence, superior to human passions. To her the prize never comes. Her languors, her dejected resumptions of life, are told with great feeling and tact, till death comes just in time to save her from the dishonour to which the *ennui* of her days had at last tempted her.

Les Deux Saints presents a curious picture
from religious life in a French country village,
the not ill-natured irony of which by no means
destroys an agreeable sense of calm remoteness
from the world in reading it.

"The little village of Champignot-les-Raisins had
an aged Curé, an old church, and in the church an
ancient image. The image was the image of St.
Vincent, patron of vine-dressers. It was of wood,
and seemed to have been shaped by the strokes of a
hatchet. It had a great belly, a big face frankly
painted with vermillion, breathing of gaiety and
good-nature—the physiognomy of a vine-dresser at
the time of vintage. Pretty it was not. But the
Curé and his flock were used to it. The image of the
good saint enjoyed the greatest consideration in the
parish, and deserved it, for it worked miracles."

The old Curé dies. His youthful successor
forces a smart new image on his flock. The
parish is divided between the votaries of the
old and the new; and the tiny provincial con-
troversy seems by a certain touch of irony to
give the true measure of many greater, perhaps
less ingenuous controversies; and for half an

hour one has a perfect calm at Champignot-les-Raisins.

M. Lemaitre writes for the most part as a pure artist. He writes to please the literary sense: to call into pleasurable exercise a delicately-formed intelligence. In one instance, however, it is to be feared he is writing for a practical purpose. *En Nourrice* describes the fate of a little child put out to nurse in the country. "He is a beautiful infant," cries the mother at his birth: "he shall be named George. I hope he may be very happy!" Alas! alas all goes the other way. His foster-brother, the strenuous Fred, wears out the frail stranger's dainty frocks—*la belle robe de Georges.* When the parents make their visits it is Fred who receives the mother's embraces instead of the pining George, sent out of sight for the occasion. In short:

"The little Parisian's destiny had been that terrible, inexplicable destiny of the infants who suffer and cry for a few months and then die, having understood nothing in it all. One night he had refused sleep. He had refused the feeding-bottle, and even the breast of Rosalie, the treat allowed him when it was too late. His eyes rolled convulsively: the cheeks were of the colour of earth: the infant was dying. Towards morning, instead of crying, little groanings had escaped him, almost like the complaints of a grown person. At last he had grown quite still and moved no more. His mother was glad to have escaped the sight of that.

"It rained in torrents when she and M. Loisil arrived at the village. The young mother, who had been in tears all the way from Paris, could weep no more, rocking herself in her damp gown, her red eyes under her crape. Early in the morning Rosalie had sent Fred to his grandmother's. She, too, was weeping,—sincerely! if you please.

"Then the mother looked at the little corpse in its cradle of basket-work. George was wearing for the first time his fine frock, dirtied by Fred. He was terribly thin, with cheeks like old wax, the nose dwindled, the eyelids blue, his tiny mouth pale and partly open, with a little foam at the back, had a touch of violet round the lips.

" 'Poor little babe! how he is changed!' said the mother, sobbing. M. Loisil looked at the dead child attentively, but said nothing. A horrible doubt had come to him.

" 'Come,' said Rosalie, 'don't look any more. It

is too painful.' Then on a sudden enters Totor, holding Fred in his arms, like a great bundle. Rosalie grew pale. Totor explained that grandmother was sick and would not keep them.

"And Fred, with one of George's caps on his head and one of George's sashes round his waist, in George's white shoes, bursting with health, good-tempered, and moving skittishly in the arms of Totor, began smiling at the lady and gentleman.

"The carpenter came, then the Curé, with a choirboy spattered with mud, carrying an old tarnished cross which tottered on its pole.

"They are sickening, those funerals of Parisian nurslings one sees sometimes crossing an empty village-street, leading, behind a coffin of the size of a violin-case, a lady and gentleman in mourning, who pass by, dabbing their eyes, while the labourers regard them curiously from the barn-doors (it happened in La Beauce) on the way to leave a bit of their own hearts in some corner of a forgotten cemetery. As the first shovel of earth fell, Madame Loisil, who had forgotten in her illness that one first kiss she had given to George, cried out, 'Ah! my poor babe, you will never have a kiss from me alive.' "

Of the *Tales Of Other Days,* two—*Boun* and *Les Funérailles de Firdousi*—are Oriental pieces, apologues, full of that mellow and tranquil wisdom which becomes the East. We profess to be no great lovers of an Oriental setting. A world from which mediæval and modern experience must, from the nature of the case, be excluded, makes on our minds an impression too vague for really artistic effect. The intimacies, the minute and concrete expression of the pathos of life, are apt to be wanting in compositions after the manner of *Rasselas*. But it is just that element—the refinement of wisdom, the refinement of justice, an exquisite compassion and mercy in the taking of life—which the reader may look for in the charming story of *Boun*.

Les Deux Fleurs is another *Story Of Other Days,* reminding us somewhat of Flaubert's *St. Julien l'Hospitalier.* Its aim is, again, that of an apologue, impressing the characteristically French moral that, "in the regard of heaven, charity is of equal value with chastity. It is best to have both if one can. Let him who lacks the second, try at all events to attain the first. Amen!" As a picture from the

Middle Ages it possesses a reality of impression not often found amid mediæval sceneries—an impression much enhanced by the gently satiric effect of the half-sceptical chaplain (a figure worthy of Chaucer), who accompanies the hero to the Crusades. Already in the Middle Ages, as he goes decorously on his way, he can divert himself in a curious observation of the ideas, the deportment of others.

"Simon Godard, mounted on his old mule, rode usually side by side with the knight-errant his master, whose candour of spirit he loved; and oftentimes they conversed together to while away the length of the journey. 'Shall we be soon in Palestine?' Sir Oy de Hautecœur asked him one day, being no great clerk in matters of geography. 'About a month hence we shall be getting near it, if no accident happens,' answered the chaplain. 'But only one-half of our number will be left when we arrive. In the East large numbers die of want, of fatigue, of malignant fevers. I don't know whether you perceive it, lost in dreaming as you always are, but we leave behind us many of our companions; and as there is no time to dig their graves, the dogs and the crows provide them another sort of sepulture.'

" 'I don't pity those,' said the knight-errant, 'who
go before us to Paradise.   The body is but a prison:
its substance vile; and it matters little what becomes
of it.'

" 'Sire, there are moments when for my part I fail
to distinguish clearly the prison from the prisoner.
It grieves me that so many of us die.   And I don't
see precisely what good end is served by their deaths.
We are spending a year and more on the work of
taking two or three towns, and when the day of
conquest comes we shall be but a handful of men.'

" 'True!   But the walls of Jericho did not fall till
the seventh day, and this is not yet the seventh
crusade.'

" 'But is it really necessary that Christians should
possess the sepulchre of the Lord, which, after all,
is an empty sepulchre, and which He suffers to remain for a thousand years in the hands of infidels?
And don't you think that the soil of their country
belongs to them, as lawfully as the soil of France
to Frenchmen?'

" 'Talk not thus, Master Chaplain: such railleries
ill become a Churchman and a holy man like yourself.'

" 'I am not joking, sire!   But the will of Heaven
does not appear to me so manifestly as it appears to
you.   It irks me to think that Heaven has given
to its worst enemies a wiser industry than ours, and

better engines of war, and the victory over its faithful servants.'

" 'Are you unaware then that their riches come from the devil and serve only to maintain them in their abominable manners? If Heaven permits them to overcome us from time to time, that is because it tries those whom it loves, because trials purify and lift us to itself.'

" 'Sire! you would make an excellent theologian and I but an indifferent knight. But if by good fortune I were a *seigneur* in the land of France, I think I should seldom leave it. While the *seigneurs* go afar to get killed, the stay-at-home fall behind with their dues. The *bourgeois* in the towns add pound to pound, and as the *seigneurs* want money for their distant expeditions, get by purchase all sorts of liberties. I don't complain of that, being of the people myself. But what I say is, that a nobleman who takes the Cross is greatly taken in.'

" 'I am aware, Master Chaplain, that you are not uttering your true thoughts, and that all this is meant to try me. I am not troubled because other Christians endeavour to improve their low and hard condition. For myself, I am neither a draper nor a grocer that I should remain always in my hole, taking no thought except for money and bodily gratification. I am in quest of what is of higher price. I am made of different paste from your *bourgeois* and your serfs. I should scarce be able to remain long in any one place, or limit my happiness to the things one can see and touch. I love the Demoiselle de Blanc-Lys, and I leave her not knowing whether I shall return. I go to make my trial in an adventure which you declare foolish and useless, and of which certainly I shall have no profit even if I succeed. And wherefore?—I know not. Only I can do no otherwise. And I have a sense that it is pleasing to God and that I am a workman of His.'

"Master Simon Godard could only answer, 'Amen!'"

On the whole, *Pauvre Ame* is the most characteristic of M. Lemaitre's shorter stories. We think the English reader will forgive some copious extracts.

"If one must needs feel pity for all people's sorrows, the life and heart of an honest man would not suffice. One would begin by lamenting the violent and tragic griefs which force themselves into view. And then those other sorrows, the sorrows which are modest, which hide themselves under a veil of sweetness and seeming serenity. There are destinies stifled and silent, where the pain is so secret and so equable in its continuance, and makes so little sound, that no one thinks of commiseration. Yet nothing

is more worthy of pity than those unquiet and soli-
tary hearts, which have yearned to give themselves
and no one has cared to take, which have lavished
their treasures unheeded and without fruit, and
which death at last carries away, outwardly intact,
but torn within, because they preyed upon themselves."

Mademoiselle de Mérisols, then, one of those
quiet souls whose fortunes M. Lemaitre loves
to trace, inhabited in an old street of convents a
small set of apartments, with melancholy old
furniture she had been able to keep from what
had belonged to her parents. The happiest
hours of her life were at the Sunday mass and
vespers. She would have been pretty could she
have felt gay. She loves and is disappointed;
but she bravely resumes once more her life of
hard work as a teacher, putting her from time
to time in contact with home scenes which only
bring the closer to herself her sense of isolation
in the world. Love comes at last, but in that
ironic mood which seems to be one of M. Lemaitre's fixed ideas of the spirit of human life.

She was thirty-five. The excellent M. de
Maucroix was twenty years older. But she
felt afraid of eternal solitude. She had hopes
of a child, but it never came. For eight years
she was her husband's nurse. She closed his
eyes and shed tears for him. She found herself
rich. Only once again the poor soul was alone
in the world. She busied herself in good works,
but felt an immense weariness. What she
needed was some one she might love singly and
with all her force. Then follows one of those
curious episodes only possible in Roman
Catholic France, and the writer finds his opportunity for a striking clerical portrait.

"Madame de Maucroix was in the habit of attend·
ing the Sunday Offices at the chapel of the Domini-
cans. It was warmer, sweeter, more intimate, than
in the churches. Many women of fashion repaired
thither, rustling softly as in a drawing-room.

"One great festival a monk preached—thirty
years of age, handsome, slender, with a superb
pallor. He talked much of love and human affections. He quoted Plato, Virgil, Lamartine. He
preached on doubt, and was still more modern. He

quoted contemporaries—Jouffroy, Leopardi, Heine,
De Musset.   He described the anguish of a mind
which does not believe; and some of his touches would
have been equally appropriate to the picture of a
heart in anguish because it does not love.   Father
Montarcy was one of those generous hearts with a
superficial mind often to be found in the order of St.
Dominic.   He had all the beautiful illusions of
Lacordaire, and united to them some pretensions to
science.   He was one of those monks who have read
Darwin and attend the physiological courses at the
Sorbonne.   His style of speaking was vague and in-
flated, but with flights of real beauty.   He moved
along, involved in his dream, isolated from what is
real, body and soul alike draped in white—draped
with much skill.   He was profoundly chaste, but
felt his power over women, taking pleasure in it in
spite of himself, lending himself to their adoration.

"He became the director of Madame de Maucroix.
She told him the story of her life and confided to him
the void in her heart.   What was she to do to fill
that void?   And every time she called him Father
bethought herself that he might have been her son.

"With a fine stroke of policy, moved also by the
poor woman's desolation, and responding to his own
secret desire, he observed gravely: 'My daughter, it
is I who should call you mother, and you shall call
me son.   I am young, and I feel how feeble I should

be without that special aid which Heaven accords to
its priests. I may believe that you have acquired by
a life of virtue an illumination equal to that con-
ferred by the holy oil of the priesthood. Will you
be my mother and director?' And he, in his turn,
confessed himself to Madame de Maucroix."

She had a son, then! Her life became a
charming one. Every morning she assisted at
his mass. She busied herself, precisely as a
mother might have done, with his wardrobe and
his linen. She accompanied him to the various
towns to which he went to preach, and listened
with delight to all his sermons. She seeks to
know the family history of Father Montarcy,
and hearing that he was an orphan feels her joy
renewed. He was the son of a working-man,
like the Saviour, like many who have become
powerful in this world. She does but admire
him the more. He had but one sister, devout,
insignificant enough, a dressmaker in a country
town. Madame de Maucroix provided a
dowry and got her well married. She feels
proud to have a hand in all the affairs of the

convent, in going thither with perfect freedom, receiving from the fathers as she passes ceremonious smiles and greetings, as if in recognition of her right.   Often she would call to mind the great Christian women of the early Church, Paula, Monica.   It was fascinating to play the part of a Mother of the Church.   What Madame Swetchine had been for Lacordaire, it was her dream to be for Father Montarcy.

Only she carried the part of director a little too far.   A kind of jealousy—jealousy of penitents younger, and with other charms than hers —mingles with her devotion.

" 'Pardon my freedom,' she says one day, 'but it is dangerous for a man of your age to listen for hours to the confessions of young women made after the manner of the one who has just left you.'

"It was like a blow in the face.   The young monk raised himself in all the pride of his priesthood, pride of a man chaste and sure of himself, with the rudeness of a monk contemptuous of women.   The chapel was empty.   He darted out of the confessional, and with a terrible voice, a magnificent tragic movement of his great sleeves, exclaimed: 'Madame de Maucroix!

Understand! I forbid you to intrude into my life as a priest and interfere in matters which concern Heaven and myself alone.' And he quitted the chapel with majestic step.

"Madame de Maucroix sank upon the pavement. Next day, broken down with grief and quite prepared to humiliate herself, she returned to the convent. The porter informed her that Father Montarcy was absent. The Prior, whom she asked to see, announced in freezing tones that he was departed for the Tyrol, where he purposed to spend some months in a convent recently founded. She understood that all was over. She possessed in Sologne a little old country-house, and thither she took refuge. There she lived for a year amid the melancholy of the pinewoods, of the violet heaths and motionless meres stained with blood at sunset, passing her days in the practice of a minute and mechanical devotion, sleepily plucking the beads of her rosary, chilled, without thoughts, with tearless eyes. In truth, she was dying day by day of an affection of the liver, aggravated suddenly by her recent emotions. When she saw that her end was near, she begged the sister who nursed her to write to Father Montarcy that she was going to die. Actually she died next day, and the Father's answer came too late. It was wanting in simplicity, though perhaps not in sincerity: 'My mother! my mother! all is forgotten.

Ah! often have I wept in the presence of Heaven,'
&c., &c.   It was signed, 'Your son.'

"The good sister, who received the letter, thought
she might open it, and felt somewhat surprised and
scandalised."

The peculiar sense of irony which is the clos-
ing effect of every one of these shorter pieces
is also the prevailing note of *Serenus*—that
more lengthy and weighty narrative, which
gives name to the whole volume.   It embodies
the imaginary confession of a supposed Christian martyr, who was not in reality a Christian
at all, who had in truth died by his own hand.

At daybreak, on a morning of March, A. D.
90, a group of Christians has come to the
Mamertine prison to receive the bodies of certain criminals condemned to death.

"It was cold: small rain was falling: towards the
east the sky was tinged with an impure and ghastly
yellow.   The Eternal City, emerging from the
shadows of night, unrolled around the Capitol its
gray billows of house, like a dirty sea after a storm.
Certain ponderous monuments rose above the rest

here and there.   Their wet roofs shone feebly in the dawn."

"Let us pray for our brothers!" says an aged priest in the company; and at that moment the magistrates entrusted with the execution of capital sentences emerge from the prison.   The Christians enter.   The head and trunk of the grey-haired consular, Flavius Clemens, are lying there.   A patch of blood glistens on the ground beside him.   One of the Christians dips in it the corner of a white linen cloth, which he folds carefully and hides within his tunic.   In the next cell lay the corpse of a man still young. He seemed to have died a natural death.   Even in death his fine but enigmatic features wore an air of irony and pride.   "The body of Marcus Annæus Serenus!" cries the gaoler.   "He was found dead this morning.   The triumvirs thought it not worth while to decapitate a dead body.   It is thought he died of poison."   The rude face of the aged priest contracted suddenly with a look of surprise, of pain and indignation.

Through the midst of the contemptuous by-standers the bodies are reverently borne away along the Appian Way, well described by **M.** Lemaitre, to a vast subterranean chamber, the tomb of Flavius Clemens, where the priest Timotheus remains alone for a time with the sacred remains. As he gazes on the face of Serenus with a look "keen and persistent, as if he would have fathomed to its depths the mysterious soul which dwelt no longer in that elegant form," his hand rests for a moment on the bosom of the corpse. He feels something below the silken tunic—a roll of parchment. He recognises the handwriting of Serenus. But the characters are small and fine, impossible to read in that feeble light. Hardly pausing to cover the pale face, he hastens from the sepulchre, and returns with the manuscript to his sordid lodging in Rome. Here he draws forth and reads with eagerness the confessions of Serenus.

"It is folly perhaps to undertake this confession. Either it will not be read, or it will distress those

who read it.   Still, it may be, that in recounting my
story to myself for the last time, I shall justify myself in my own eyes.   Some worthy souls have loved
me, but none have really known me.   Now, though
for a long time past it has been my pride to live in
myself, to be impenetrable to every one beside, my
secret weighs upon me to-day.   A certain regret
comes to me (it is almost remorse) that I have played
so successfully the singular part which circumstances and my own curiosity have imposed upon me;
and I should wish, by way of persuading myself that
I could not have acted otherwise, to take up the
entire chain of my thoughts and actions from my
earliest days to the day on which I am to die."

It is a charming figure, certainly, which
Serenus displays, rich with intellectual endow-
ments, and a heart that, amid all the opportu-
nities for corruption which could beset a fortunate patrician in the days of Domitian, never
loses its purity to the last—affectionate, reflective, impressible by pity, with "the gift of
tears."   And here is one of his earliest experiences.

"I was twelve years old when the great fire
,destroyed one-half of Rome and threw more than a

hundred thousand people on the pavements. During two or three years, in spite of the enormous distributions of money and bread ordered by the emperor, the misery in Rome was fearful. The spectacle of so much undeserved suffering wounded my heart incurably. I conceived a lively notion of the injustice cf things and the absurdity of men's destinies. I found it unjust that my father should be the possessor of five hundred slaves while so many poor people were dying of hunger. I gave away all the money I could dispose of. But, with the stiff logic of my age, I considered that no thanks were due to me, and avoided people's effusive thanks, the coarseness of which shocked the fine taste of my aristocratic youth. One day my tutor took me to a grand festival which Nero gave to the people in his gardens. To divert the anger of the populace, which accused him of being the author of the conflagration, he had caused some hundreds of Christians to be arrested. The majority of them had been thrown to the beasts in the circus: others, arrayed in sacks steeped in resin, were attached to tall stakes at intervals along the broad pathways. At nightfall fire was applied to them. The crowds pressed with loud vociferations around the living torches. The flame which enveloped the culprits, hollowed by the wind from time to time, allowed the horrible faces to be seen, with great open mouths,

though one could not hear the cries. A stench of
burnt flesh filled the air. I had a nervous attack
and was carried home half dead. The shock had
been too great; and although at that age the most
painful impressions are quickly effaced, something
of it remained with me—a languor of spirit at certain
moments, a melancholy, an indolence of pulse, rare in
a child."

This was on one side: on the other were the
varied intellectual interests offered to a reflective mind in that curious, highly educated, wist-
ful age. In a few effective but sparing traits
Serenus depicts his intellectual course, through
the noble dreams of a chaste Stoicism, through
the exquisite material voluptuousness of Epicureanism when the natural reaction had come,
until, having exhausted experience, as he fan-
cies, he proposes to die.

It was an age in which people had carried the
art of enjoyment to its height.

"Never before, I think, has the world seen, never
again will it see, so small a number of persons absorb
and occupy for their own uses so large a number
of human lives. Some of my friends had as many

as three thousand slaves, and hardly knew the real
extent of their riches.   And the science of pleasure
was on a level with the resources at its disposition.
Many successive generations of a privileged class
had made a study of the means of refining, varying,
multiplying, agreeable sensations.   Posterity, as-
suredly, will hardly conceive the kind of life which
some of us have known and practised.   But as the
future will not easily imagine the intensity of our
physical pleasures, perhaps it will even less understand the depth of our satiety.   It will be surprised,
in reading our chronicles, at the number of those
who in this age have committed suicide.   After
fifteen years of a revel, refined and coarse by turns,
my body exhausted, my senses dulled, my heart void
to the bottom of all belief, and even of illusion, what
was I to do in the world?   It figured to me as a
ridiculous spectacle, and interested me no longer.   I
had retained that native sweetness of temper which
came to me from my father, but only because I found
it pleasant to be kind; and even that too was come
to be indifferent to me.   For the rest, public employ-
ments had become sordid things of purchase, and I
loathed every form of activity.   I languished in an
immense, an incurable *ennui*, and having no further
motive to live, I wished to die.   Death had no fears
for me.   It was the great deliverer.   Only, I desired
to die without suffering."

The would-be suicide is saved from death by
the intervention, at the last moment, of his
sister, the youthful Serena, in the retired life
of a young orphan girl scarcely known by him
hitherto; and her subsequent devotion during
the long illness which follows touches him
deeply. In reality her devotion is due in part
to a motive higher than natural sisterly devotion. On the part of Serenus also, there was
something deeper than merely fraternal affection.

"It was love of a peculiar kind, such as I had never
before experienced in the faintest degree. Serena
was so different from all the women I had ever known.
It seemed to me that that love evoked from the
depths of my past life and brought to new birth
within me what had been lost in my earlier days,
those ardours of the youthful sage aspiring towards
an absolute purity. Then, in proportion as I re-
covered my mental vigour, my old curiosity returned; and little by little I introduced into this
ardent affection for my sister, the attentive mood of
an observer, attracted by the spectacle of an extraordinary soul.

"One day Serena said to me, 'Will you give me a

great pleasure?   Come with me to-morrow morning
where I shall take you.'

" 'I will go where you will, Serena.' "

Serena takes him to see the ceremonies of the
Eucharist in a Christian oratory.

"I perceived among the company assembled the
consul of that year, Flavius Clemens—a circumstance which explained the fact that this meeting
took place in one of the burial places of his family.
I recognised the wife of Clemens and his niece, and
Paulina, the widow of Seneca, pale for ever from having followed her husband more than half way on the
road to death.   They were deeply veiled.   At last I
saw in the front rank Acte, the former mistress of
Nero, the former friend of my father, still beautiful
in spite of her fifty years, but with a little of the
cosmetic art, methinks.   The rest of the company
appeared to be composed of poor people and slaves."

To Serenus the company, the office for which
it was assembled, seemed grave, majestic,
touching, and something altogether new.   But
he perceives also, clearly enough, once for all,
that for him these rites will never be more than
a spectacle, that there is a gulf between these
people and himself.

" 'My dear Serenus,' said my sister, as we departed, 'you have now seen what the Christians are. You will love them more and more in proportion as you come to know them. You are unhappy, as I well know. You must become a Christian. The Truth is there. There, also, is the secret of consolation.'

" 'I will think of it, Serena.' "

In fact, he takes pains to inform himself on the matter, interested at finding many a familiar thought of ancient pagan wisdom in a new setting. Yes!—

"All the virtues which the pagan philosophers had already known and preached seemed to me among the disciples of Christ to have been transformed by a sentiment absolutely new—a love of a God who was man, a God crucified—a love burning, full of sensibility, of tears, of confidence, of hope. Clearly, neither the personification of the forces of nature, nor the abstract deity of the Stoics, had ever inspired anything like this. And this love of God, the origin of, and first step towards, all other Christian virtues, communicated to them a purity and sweetness, an unction, and, as it were, a perfume, such as I had never breathed before."

Yet with all his heartfelt admiration for believers, Serenus is still unable to believe.   Like
a creature of the nineteenth century he finds the
world absolutely subject to the reign of physical law.   And then there were difficulties of
another sort, of which he became sensible now
and again.

"The idea which my new brethren entertained of
the world about us, and of our life here, jarred upon
I know not what sentiment of nature within me.   In
spite of my own persistent pessimism, I was dis-
pleased that men should so despise the only mode of
life, after all, of which we are certain.   I found
them, moreover, far too simple-minded, closed
against all artistic impressions, limited, inelegant.
Or, perhaps, a certain anxiety awaking in me, I
feared for the mischief which might be caused to the
empire by a conception of life such as that, if it
continued to spread—a detachment such as theirs
from all civil duties, all profane occupations.   Sometimes I was decidedly unjust to them.   The religious
after-thought which the Christians mingled with
their affections, by way of purifying them, seemed
to me to chill those affections, in depriving them of
their natural liberty, their grace, their spontaneity.
To be loved only as redeemed by Christ, and in regard

of my eternal salvation, made my heart cold. And then it shocked me that these saintly people should feel so sure of so many things, and things so wonderful, while I, for my part, had searched so carefully without finding, had doubted so much in my life, and finally made a pride of my unbelief."

But, inconsistently enough, he is offended at times by the survival of many a human weakness among the believers. The consul Clemens, among those brothers who were all equal before Heaven, was treated with marked consideration, and welcomed it. Slaves were still slaves. The women were rivals for the special attention of the priests. Acte, once the mistress of Nero, somewhat exaggerated her piety, and still retained also many of her former artificial manners.

"In spite of those little weaknesses, what good, what beautiful souls, I came across there! In vain I said to myself, these holy persons are making a bargain; they reckon on Paradise; it is in view of a reward that they practise the most sublime virtues. But to believe at all in that distant far-off recompense, is not this too itself an act of virtue, since it

involves belief in the justice of God, and a conception of Him, as being that which He ought to be?"

And noting sometimes the ardent quality of
their faith and its appropriateness to human
needs, the needs especially of the poor and suffering, Serenus could not but feel that the
future would be with them. If the empire
failed, the religion of Christ would flourish on
its ruins. Then, what sort of a thing would
that new humanity be? More virtuous, doubtless, and therefore happier, since happiness
comes of the soul; on the other hand, he thinks
(mistakenly, as we know, looking backwards
on the length and breadth of Christian history)
with less art, and less elegance of soul, a feebler
understanding of the beautiful.

Presently, a certain change takes place in
the life of the Christian community. The influence of Calixtus, a priest of the sweeter and
more lenient type, is superseded by that of
Timotheus, lately returned to Rome—a man
sincerely good, but narrow-minded and rigor-
ous in his zeal. He would have Serenus receive

baptism, or depart entirely from the church.
It takes Serenus some time to explain away his
scruples regarding what seems at first sight an
act of hypocrisy. And then the trial comes.
Partly on the ground of their religious belief,
mainly for an affront to the Emperor, the chief
members of the community are arrested.
Serenus has said adieu to his sister. He is in
prison, awaiting his end.

"My gaoler is a good-natured fellow. I had about
me the means of writing, and he has procured me a
lamp. He informs me that the executioner will come
about the hour of daybreak. I have been writing
all the night. My last link to life is broken! and
death, be it annihilation, be it the passage to a
world unknown, has no terrors for me. I have replaced myself almost exactly in the state of mind in
which I was last year, when I determined to die in my
bath. But at this last moment a dread has come
upon me for a death which soils and disfigures: I fear
the stroke of the axe, which may fail in its aim. In
my time the science of poisons has reached a high
perfection, and the hollow pearl in my ring contains
a colourless drop of liquid which will destroy me in a
few minutes, almost without pain. I have seen the

honours Christians pay to the burial-place wherein
rest the remains of the victims of Nero. They will
honour me also as one of their saints. Can I, at this
late hour, undeceive them? But for what purpose?
I am willing they should guess the fact of my suicide,
that they should read my confession; yet I will do
nothing to that end; for if Serena knew how I died,
in what condition of unbelief, her grief would be too
great for her. For the rest, I have good hope that
Timotheus, who has no love for me, will allow only a
limited form of reverence to be paid to my bones;
and if some simple hearts revere me more than I
deserve, again what does it matter? It is their faith
will be reckoned to them, not the merits of the saint
they will invoke. And then, after all, it is not a bad
man whose memory they will honour. I have sincerely sought for truth. I forced myself in youth to
attain to sanctity as I conceived it. And if I have
been indolent, weak, voluptuous—if I have done little
for other people—at least I have always had great
indulgence for them, a great pity."

The austere Timotheus, full of suspicion,
pored for hours over the manuscript, which was
clear enough at the beginning. But the schol-
arly Latin of the young patrician was not always intelligible to him, towards the end the

handwriting became confused, and he remained still in doubt regarding the precise character of the death of Serenus. He might have confided the confession to a more expert reader; but, though profoundly curious on the matter, he feared a possible scandal. More than suspicious, he would fain allow Serenus the benefit of such doubt as remained. If he had not died for Christ, at least he had been condemned because of Him; and, perhaps, even at the last moment, some sudden illumination, some gleam of faith had come to him. For a moment he thought of burning the manuscript; but a certain sense of respect for the dead restrained him. He replaced the manuscript in the fold of the tunic: "Let his sin, or his innocence, remain with him. God! who judgest the heart, I recommend my brother to your goodness!"

It is about eight hundred years later that we find Serenus again—Marcus Annæus Serenus, by the designation of his tombstone in the catacombs,—as Saint Marc le Romain, at Beau-

gency-sur-Loire, whither his precious relics
have been brought from Rome by the Abbot
Angelran. Among those relics the Abbot had
discovered the manuscript, and confided it, still
intact, to the most learned member of the
Benedictine community over which he presided.
With him those old doubts of Timotheus became certainty. With much labour he de-
ciphers the writing, and discovers that the supposed martyr had died a pagan.

But Saint Marc the Roman had already become popular, and worked miracles. The
learned monk was unwilling to trouble the
minds of the faithful, to gratify, moreover, the
monks of a rival house. Still, he lacked the
courage to destroy a document so singular, and
hid the manuscript in a corner of the monastic
library. It passed we are told, in 1793, into the
public library of Beaugency, where it was
found and read by our author.

The reputation of Saint Marc the Roman
maintained itself till far onwards in the Middle
Ages. His miracles, like himself of old,

were always considerate, always full of "indulgence."

The same sort of irony, then, makes itself felt, as the final impression of the history of Serenus—the same sort of irony as that which shaped the fortunes of M. Lemaitre's other characters—the worthiest of all the sisters, who fails to get married: the mother who embraces the wrong infant: Boun, with her gift of the fairy's ring, whose last, best miracle of assistance is but to restore her again to the simplicity of mind and body in which it had found her. "She has this irony—Dame Nature!"—and in the recognition of it, supplemented by a keen sense of what should be the complementary disposition on man's part, is the nearest approach which our author makes to a philosophy of life. Nature, circumstance, is far from pitiful, abounds in mockeries, in baffling surprises and misadventures, like a cynical person amused with the distresses of children. Over against that cynical humour, it may be our part to promote in life the mood of the kindly person, still regarding people very much as children, but, like Serenus, with "a great pity for them, a great indulgence."

M. Lemaitre has many and varied interests, a marked individuality of his own amid them all, and great literary accomplishments. His success in the present volume might well encourage him to undertake a work of larger scope,—to add to his other excellent gifts, in the prolonged treatment of some one of those many interests, that great literary gift of patience.

THE LIFE AND LETTERS OF
GUSTAVE FLAUBERT[1]

PROSE as a fine art, of which French literature affords a continuous illustration, had in Gustave Flaubert, a follower, unique in the decisiveness of his conception of that art and the disinterestedness of his service to it. Necessitated by weak health to the regularity and the quiet of a monk, he was but kept the closer to what he had early recognised as his vocation in life. By taking care, he lived to be almost sixty years old, in the full use of his gift, as we may suppose, and he wrote seven or eight books, none of them lengthy. "Neglect nothing," he writes to a friend. "Labour! Do the thing over again, and don't leave your work till you

---

[1] Correspondance—Première Série 1830-1850 (Paris).

feel convinced that you have brought it to the
last point of perfection possible for you. In
these days genius is not rare. But what no one
has now, what we should try to have, is the conscience of one's work." To that view he was
faithful; and he had and keeps his reward. So
sparing as a writer of books, he was a volumin-
ous letter writer. A volume of his letters to
George Sand appeared in 1883. In 1887 his
niece, for many years his intimate companion,
published the first portion of his general correspondence, and it is the purpose of this paper
to note some of the lights thrown by it on himself and on his work.

Gustave Flaubert was born at Rouen in
1821. His earliest home was in the old
Maison-Dieu of which his father was surgeon.
The surgeon's household was self-respecting,
affectionate, refined, liberal in expense; but the
inevitable associations of the place—the suffering, white-capped faces at the windows—
stayed by the susceptible lad, and passed into
his work as a somewhat overbalanced sense of

unhappiness in things.   More cheerful influences came with the purchase of a country
house at Croisset, a few miles down the Seine,
on the right bank, "white and in the old style."
In after years Flaubert delighted to believe
that Pascal, that great master of prose, had
once visited it.   It was here, in the large rooms,
the delightful garden, with views of Rouen, the
busy river, the wooded hills, that the remainder
of Flaubert's life was chiefly spent.   His
letters show that the feeling of vocation to literature came early; oddly enough, for he was
no precocious child, and took a longer time
than is usual in learning to read.   From the
first he was abundant in enthusiasm for the literary art of others.   In early youth he meets
Victor Hugo, and is surprised to find him much
like any one else externally, wondering at "the
greatness of the treasure contained in so ordinary a casket," fixing his eyes devoutly "on the
right hand which had written so many beautiful things."   He was a singularly beautiful
child and records that royal ladies had stopped

their carriages to take him in their arms and
kiss him. By its vigour and beauty, again, his
youth made people think of the young demi-
gods of Greek sculpture. Then, somewhere in
early manhood, came an alarm regarding
health, both bodily and mental; and from that
time to his death he continued more or less of
an invalid, or at least a valetudinarian, enjoy-
ing life, indeed, its work, its gift, but always
with an undercurrent of nervous distress. "To
practical life," he writes at twenty-four, "I
have said an irrevocable adieu. Hence, for a
long time to come, all I ask is five or six hours
of quiet in my own room daily, a big fire in the
winter and two candles every evening to give
me light"; again, "I am well enough, now that
I have consented to be always ill"; and again,
"My life seems arranged now after a regular
plan, with less large, less varied horizons,
but the deeper perhaps, because more restrained. You would not believe what mischief
any sort of derangement causes me." Henceforth a sort of sacerdotal order is impressed

everywhere. In the quiet house his writing
table is before him, reverently covered with all
its apparatus of work, under a light silken
cloth, when a visitor is announced: his life slides
early into even grooves; an organization natur-
rally exquisite becomes fastidious. He was
still, at carefully guarded hours, abundant in
friendship, in the good humour, and the
humour or wit which attaches and amuses
friends. After all, there was plenty of
laughter, not always satiric, in his life. And
then an intimate domestic affection, so largely
evidenced in these letters, making heavy de-
mands from time to time on his patience, his
self-denial, and procuring him in return immense consideration, was a necessity alike of
his personal and his literary life. It is a very
human picture, with average battles and sorrows and joys, quite like those of the *bourgeois*
he so greatly despised, but for him with all the
joys also, all the various intellectual adventure,
of the artistic life, followed loyally as an end in
itself. The quiet people he quietly loves are a

relaxation from the somewhat over-intent character of his "art" while they supply some of its
motives. And the enforced monotony of a
recluse life is in their favour. "To take pleasure in a place it is necessary to have lived there
long. One day is not enough for warming
one's nest."

Yet in spite of bad health, in spite of his love
of retirement, of routine, his passion for a recluse life, he had been, at least for a French-
man, a good deal of a traveller. Foreign travel
—mental, and as far as might be physical
journeys, journeys—to the old classical lands,
the desert, the wondrous East, the very matter
of his work was in considerable measure de-
pendent upon that. Rapid yet penetrative
notice of the places he visits animates his correspondence. The student of his writings—so
brief a list!—is glad to add to them the record
of a journey to Brittany in 1847, written in
"collaboration" with his travelling companion,
M. Maxine du Camp. He visited many parts
of France, above all, the grand old pagan

towns of the South, Switzerland, Italy, Corsica "a brave country still virgin as to the *bourgeois* who have not yet arrived to degrade it with their admiration, a country ardent and grave, all red and black." At last with a thousand daily solicitudes for the poor old mother left at Croisset, came his long journey to Syria and Egypt, the record of which fills the last hundred pages of the volume before us.

Flaubert's first great trouble came in his twenty-fifth year, on the death of his father, followed quickly by that of his favourite sister Caroline:

"It was yesterday at eleven o'clock we interred her—poor damsel! They put her in her wedding-gown, with bunches of roses, violets and immortelles. I passed the whole night watching beside her. She lay straight, reposed on her couch, in the room where you have heard her play. She looked taller and handsomer than in life, with the long white veil down to the feet. In the morning, when all was ready, I gave her a last kiss in her coffin. I stopped down, placed my head within, felt the lead bend under my hands. It was I who had the cast taken. I saw the coarse hands handle her and enclose her in the plaster. I shall possess her hand and her face. Pradier will make the bust for me, to be placed in my own room. I have kept for myself her large striped shawl, a lock of her hair, the table and the desk at which she wrote. And that is all!—all that remains of those one has loved. . . . When we got up there in the cemetery behind the walls of which we used to go out walking in my school days, the grave was too narrow; the coffin would not go in. They shook it, pulled it this way and that, used spade and levers, and at last a gravedigger tramped upon it—where the head was—to force it into its place. I felt dried up—like the marble of a tomb—but terribly irritated. And now, since Sunday, we are at home again at Croisset. What a journey it was! alone with my mother and the infant, which cried. The last time I left, it was with yourself, you will remember. Of the four persons who then lived there two remain. . . . My mother is better than she might be; occupies herself with her daughter's babe, is trying to make herself a mother once more. Will she succeed? The reaction has not yet come and I dread it. I am crushed, stupefied. If I could but resume my tranquil life of art, of long-continued meditation!"

What note of dismay, of a kind of frozen

grief, of a capacity for pity of those resources to be so largely tested by *Madame Bovary!*

"I am prepared for everything. I am like the pavement on the high road; misfortune tramps over me as it wills." "As for me, my eyes are dry as marble. Strange. The more expansive I find myself, blind and abundant, in fictitious griefs, just in that proportion do the real griefs stay fixed in my heart, acrid and hard. They turn to crystal, there, one by one, as they come."

It is the daughter of that favourite sister who has now appeared as the editor of his letters from the year 1830 to 1850. She has introduced them by a sketch of his life which the student of Flaubert's work will value, for she became in her turn her uncle's intimate companion, and has recorded some characteristic counsels to herself, the mature experience of his artistic life applied to the formation of the mind of a young girl. "When you take up a book," he would say, "you must swallow it at one mouthful. That is the only way to know it in its entirety. Accustom yourself to follow out an idea. I don't wish you should have that loose character in your thoughts which is the appanage of persons of your sex." The author of *Salammbo* taught her ancient history. "I interrupted him sometimes," she tells us, "by the question 'Was he a good man?—Cambyses, Alexander, Alcibiades.' 'Faith, they were not very accommodating members of society— *messieurs très commodes.* But what has that to do with you?'" He went to church with her, for the young French girl could not go alone— amazing complaisance it seemed in so marked a Freethinker—awaiting, patiently, we must not be too sure with what kind of thoughts, till her duties were over.

La Bovary!—many a time she heard of that before she had any notion what the name meant. "I had a vague belief that it was a synonym for labour, perpetual labour. I assisted, a motionless witness, at the slow crea- tion of these pages so severely elaborated." There he sat, month after month, seeking, sometimes with so much pain, the expression, "the phrase," weighing the retention or rejec-

tion of an epithet—his one fixed belief the belief in beauty, literary beauty, with liberal delight at beauty in other men's work, remember-
ing after many years the precise place on the
page of some approved form of sentence. He
knew his favourite passage in Scripture, "How
beautiful upon the mountains are the feet of
them that bring glad tidings!" "Reflect on that,
get to the bottom of it, if you can," he would
say to me, full of enthusiasm.

His "distractions" were limited to certain
short absences in Paris for a day or two, about
once in three months—*pour me retremper.*
On the rare occasion, of a longer visit it was
necessary that his home companions should go
with him; and then, on certain days, his rooms
in the Boulevard du Temple were put in flow-
ery array, and he entertained a select party of
friends. "Whenever I re-enter Paris," he
writes, "I breathe at my ease." But in truth
he abhorred change. "Man is so poor a ma-
chine that a straw among the wheels spoils it."
"I live like a Carthusian," he says. Again:

"I am but a lizard, a literary lizard, warming himself all day long at the full sun of the beautiful." "For writing," his niece tells us "he required extreme tension of mind, and he never found himself in the desired condition save in his own workroom, seated at his great round table, sure that nothing could come to disturb him. He had a passionate love of order and ate sparingly. His force of will in all that concerned his 'art' was immense." He troubled himself little about "moments of inspiration," the waiting on which he held to be a cause of "sterility." Get the habit of working in ordinary daylight, and then perhaps the ray of heavenly light may come. At times the monotony of his method of life, a monotony likely to continue to the end, weighed on the spirits, especially as the passing footsteps about him grew rarer and memory took the place of sensation; for in spite of what people say,"memories don't fill one's house they do but enlarge its solitude. There is now a multitude of places at which my heart bleeds as I pass. It seems

to me," he writes—only in his twenty-fifth year
—"that the angles of my life are worn down
under the friction of all that has passed over
it."

So his life continued to the last, as he
had foreseen, somewhat painfully disturbed
towards the end by the German war. That
its barbarities should have been the work of a
literary, a scientific people, was but the last expression of a soul of stupidity in things, to his
view unmistakable. The invaders in occupa-
tion of Rouen made use of his house, but re-
spectfully. The end came in 1880, and found
him at work, alone apparently, in his large
study, with the five windows and wide views
where he had lived so long.

Madame Commanville has printed these letters chiefly because she thought they revealed
her uncle under a different light from that of
his books. A kind of scandal attached to his
writings, and the editor of his correspondence
is certainly right in thinking that her own
reminiscences of his life would, after all, make

people esteem him as a man. In truth, life and letters alike reveal him not otherwise than as we divine him through his books—the passionate, labouring, conscientious artist, who has found affection and temperance indispensable to his art, abounding in sympathy for the simple people who came nearest to him, conscious of an immense mental superiority to almost every one, a superiority which kept him high and clean in all things, yet full of pity, of practical consideration for men and women as they must be. Anxious to think him a good man, his niece, with some costly generous acts known to herself in memory, was struck above all by that tranquil devotion to art which seemed to have had about it something of the "seriousness and passion that are like a consecration"—something of religion.

"CORRESPONDANCE DE GUSTAVE FLAUBERT"

Deuxième Série (1850-54) (Paris: Charpentier)

THE second volume of Gustave Flaubert's correspondence, just now published, is even richer than the first, alike in those counsels of literary art Flaubert was preeminently fitted to give, and in lights, direct and indirect, on his own work. The letters belong to a short period in his life, from his twenty-eighth to his thirty-second year, (1850-54), during which he was an exceptionally expansive correspondent, but otherwise chiefly occupied in the composition of *Madame Bovary,* a work of immense labour, as also of great and original genius. The more systematic student might draw from these letters many an interesting paragraph to add, by way of foot-notes, to that impressive book.

The earlier letters find Flaubert still in the East, recording abundantly those half-savage notes of ancient civilisation which are in sympathy with the fierce natural colouring of the country he loved so well. The author of *Salammbo* and *Herodias* is to be detected already in this lively vignette from an Oriental square:

"Nothing is more graceful than the spectacle of all those men (the Dervishes) waltzing, with their great petticoats twisted, their ecstatic faces lifted to the sky. They turn, without a moment's pause, for about an hour. One of them assured us that, if he were not obliged to hold his hands above his head, he could turn for six hours continuously."

Even here, then, it is the calm of the East which expresses itself—the calm, perhaps the emptiness, of the Oriental, of which he has fixed the type in the following sketch:

"I have seen certain dancing girls, who balanced themselves with the regularity of a palm tree. Their eyes, of a profound depth, express calm only—nothing but the calm, the emptiness, of the desert. It is the same with the men. What admirable heads! heads which seem to be turning over within them the grandest thoughts in the world. But tap on them! and there will be only the empty beer-glass, the deserted sepulchre. Whence then the majesty of their eternal form? of what does it really hold? Of the absence, I should reply, of all passion. They have the beauty of the ruminating ox, of the grey-hound in its race, the floating eagle—that sentiment of fatality which is fulfilled in these. A conviction of the nothingness of man gives to all they do, their looks, their attitudes, a resigned but grandiose character. Their loose and easy raiment, lending itself freely to every movement of the body, is always in closest accord with the wearer and his functions; with the sky, too, by its colour; and then the sun! There is an immense *ennui* there in the sun, which consumes everything.''

But it is as brief essays in literary criticism that these letters are most effective. Exquisitely personal essays, self-explanatory, or by way of confession, written almost exclusively to one person—a perfectly sympathetic friend, engaged like the writer in serious literary work —they possess almost the unity, the connected current of a book. It is to Madame X., however, that Flaubert makes this cynical admission about women:

"What I reproach in women, above all, is their need of *poetisation,* of forcing poetry into things. A man may be in love with his laundress, but will know that she is stupid, though he may not enjoy her company the less. But if a woman loves her inferior, he is straightway an unrecognised genius, a superior soul, or the like. And to such a degree does this innate disposition to see crooked prevail, that women can perceive neither truth when they encounter it, nor beauty where it really exists. This fault is the true cause of the deceptions of which they so often complain. To require oranges of apple trees is a common malady with them."

Flaubert, as seen in these letters, was undoubtedly a somewhat austere lover. His true mistress was his art. Counsels of art there are—for the most part, the best thing he has to offer. Only rarely does he show how he could play the lover:

"Your love, penetrates me at last, like warm rain, and I feel myself searched through with it, to the bottom of my heart. Have you not everything that could make me love you? body, wit, tenderness? You

are simple of soul and strong of head; not poetic,
yet a poet in extreme degree.   There is nothing but
good in you: and you are wholly, as your bosom is,
white, and soft to touch.   I try sometimes to fancy
how your face will look when you are old, and it
seems to me I shall love you still as much as now,
perhaps more."

In contrast with the majority of writers, apt
to make a false pretence of facility, it is of his
labour that Flaubert boasts.   That was because, after all, labour did but set free the innate lights of a true diamond; it realised, was a
ministry to, the great imaginative gift of which
he was irresistibly conscious.   It was worth his
while!

"As for me, the more I feel the difficulties of good
writing, the more my boldness grows.   It is this
preserves me from the pedantry into which I should
otherwise fall.   I have plans for books, the composition of which would occupy the rest of my life; and
if there happen to me, sometimes, cruel moments,
which well-nigh make me weep with anger (so great
do I feel my weakness to be), there are others also
when I can scarce contain myself for joy: something
from the depth within me, for which voluptuous is no

word, overflows for me in sudden leaps. I feel transported, almost inebriate, with my own thoughts, as if there came to me, at some window within, a puff of warm perfumes. I shall never go very far, and know how much I lack; but the task I undertake will surely be executed by another. I shall have put on the true road some one better endowed, better born, for the purpose, than myself. The determination to give to prose the rhythm of verse, leaving it still veritable prose; to write the story of common life as history or the epic gets written (that is to say, without detriment to the natural truth of the subject), is perhaps impossible. I ask myself the question sometimes. Yet it is perhaps a considerable, an original thing, to have tried. I shall have had my permanent value for my obstinacy. And who knows? One day I may find a good *motif*, and air entirely within the compass of my voice; and at any rate I shall have passed my life not ignobly, often with delight. Yet still it is saddening to think how many great men arrive easily at the desired effect, by means beyond the limits of conscious art. What could be worse built than many things in Rabelais, Cervantes, Molière, Hugo? But, then, what sudden thrusts of power! What power in a single word!"

Impersonality in art, the literary ideal of Gustave Flaubert, is perhaps no more possible

than realism.   The artist *will* be felt; his sub-
jectivity must and will colour the incidents, as
his very bodily eye *selects* the aspects of things.
By force of an immense and continuous effort,
however, the whole scope of which these letters
enabled us to measure, Flaubert did keep *Madame Bovary* at a great distance from himself; the author might be thought to have been
completely hidden out of sight in his work.
Yet even here he transpires, clearly enough,
from time to time; and the morbid sense of life,
everywhere impressed in the very atmosphere
of that sombre history, came certainly of the
writer himself.   The cruelty of the way of
things—that is a conviction of which the development is partly traceable in these letters.

"Provided the brain remains!   That is the chief
thing.   But how nothingness invades us!   We are
scarcely born ere decay begins for us, in such a way
that the whole life is but one long combat with it,
more and more triumphant, on its part, to the con-
sumation, namely, death; and then the reign of decay
is exclusive.   There have been at most two or three
years in which I was really entire—from seventeen to

nineteen. I was splendid just then, though I scarcely like to say so now; enough to attract the eyes of a whole assembly of spectators, as happened to me at Rouen, on the first presentation of *Ruy Blas.* Ever since then I have deteriorated—at a furious pace. There are mornings when I feel afraid to look at myself, so worn and used-up am I grown."

Madame Bovary, of course, was a tribute to science; and Flaubert had no dread, great hopes rather, of the service of science in imaginative literature, though the combat between scientific truth—mental physiology and the like—and that perfectly finished academic style he preferred, might prove a hard one. We might be all of us, since Sophocles—well, "tattooed savages!" but still, there was "something else in art besides rectitude of line and the well-polished surface." The difficulty lay in the limitations of language, which it would be the literary artist's true contention to enlarge. "We have too many things, too few words. 'Tis from that comes the torture of the fine literary conscience." But it was one's duty, none the less, to accept all, "imprint all,

and, above all, fix one's *point d'appui* in the
present." Literature, he held, would take
more and more the modes of action which now
seem to belong exclusively to science. It would
be, above all, *exposante*—by way of exposition;
by which, he was careful to point out, he by no
means intended *didactic*. One must make pictures, by way of showing nature as she really
is; only, the pictures must be complete ones.
We must paint both sides, the upper and
under. Style—what it might be, if writers
faithfully cherished it—that was the subject of
his perpetual consideration. Here is a sketch
of the prose style of the future:

"Style, as I conceive it, style as it will be realised
some day—in ten years, or ten generations! It
would be rhythmical as verse itself, precise as the
language of science; and with undulations—a swell-
ing of the violin! plumage of fire! A style which
would enter into the idea like the point of a lancet;
when thought would travel over the smooth surfaces
like a canoe with fair winds behind it. Prose is but
of yesterday, it must be confessed. Verse is *par ex-
cellence* the form of the ancient literatures. All

possible prosodic combinations have been already made; those of prose are still to make."

The effort, certainly, cost him much; how much we may partly see in these letters, the more as *Madame Bovary,* on which he was then mainly at work, made a large demand also on his impersonality:

"The cause of my going so slowly is just this, that nothing in that book (*Madame Bovary*) is drawn from myself. Never has my personality been so useless to me. It may be, perhaps, that hereafter I shall do stronger things. I hope so, but I can hardly imagine I shall do anything more skilful. Here everything is of the head. If it has been false in aim, I shall always feel that it has been a good mental exercise. But after all, what is the non-natural to others is the natural to me—the extraordinary, the fantastic, the wild chase, mythologic, or metaphysic. *Saint Antoine* did not require of me one quarter of the tension of mind *Madame Bovary* has caused me. *Saint Antoine* was a discharge; I had nothing but pleasure in writing it; and the eighteen months devoted to the composition of its five hundred pages were the most thoroughly voluptuous of my life, hitherto. Judge them, of my condition in writing *Madame Bovary.* I must needs put myself every minute into a skin not mine, and antipathetic to me. For six months now I have been making love Platonically; and at the present moment my exaltation of mind is that of a good Catholic: I am longing to go to confession."

A constant reader of Montaigne, Flaubert pushed to the utmost the habit of doubt, as leading to artistic detachment from all practical ends:

"Posterity will not be slow in cruel desertion of those who have determined to be useful, and have sung for a cause. It cares very little for Château-briand, and his resuscitation of mediæval religion; for Béranger, with his libertine philosophy; will soon care little for Lamartine and his religious humanitarianism. Truth is never in the present; and if one attaches oneself to the present, there comes an end of one. At the present moment, I believe that even a thinker (and the artist, surely, is three times a thinker) should have no convictions."

Flaubert himself, whatever we may think of that, had certainly attained a remarkable degree of detachment from the ordinary interests of mankind.

Over and above its weightier contributions to the knowledge of Flaubert, to the knowledge and practice of literature at its best, this volume, like its predecessor, abounds in striking occasional thoughts:

"There is no imagination in France. If you want to make real poetry pass, you must be clever enough to disguise it."

"In youth one associates the future realisation of one's dreams with the existence of the actual people around us. In proportion as those existences disappear, our dreams also depart."

"Nothing is more useless than those heroic friendships which require exceptional circumstances to prove them. The great difficulty is to find some one who does not rack your nerves in every one of the various ordinary occurrences of life."

"The dimensions of a soul may be measured by its power of suffering, as we calculate the depth of rivers by their current."

"Formerly, people believed that the sugar-cane alone yielded sugar; nowadays it is extracted from almost anything. It is the same with poetry. Let us draw it, no matter whence, for it lies everywhere, and in all things. Let us habituate ourselves to regard the world as a work of art, the processes of which are to be reproduced in our works."

"To have talent, one must be convinced one has it; and to keep the conscience pure, we must put it above the consciences of all other people."

"We retain always a certain grudge against any one who instructs us."

"What is best in art will always escape people of mediocrity, that is to say, more than three quarters of the human race."

"Let our enemies speak evil of us! it is their proper function. It is worse when friends speak well of us foolishly."

"Materialists and spiritualists, in about equal degree, prevent the knowledge of matter and spirit alike, because they sever one from the other. The one party make man an angel, the other a swine."

"In proportion as it advances, art will be more and more scientific, even as science will become artistic. The two will rejoin each other at the summit, after separating at the base."

"Let us be ourselves, and nothing else! 'What is your duty? What each day requires.' That is Goethe's notion. Let *us* do our duty; which is, to try to write well. What a society of saints we should be. if only each one of us did his duty."

COLERIDGE AS A THEOLOGIAN

COLERIDGE had designed an intellectual novelty in the shape of a religious philosophy. Socinian theology and the philosophy of Hartley had become distasteful. "Whatever is against right reason, that no faith can oblige us to believe." Coleridge quotes these words from Jeremy Taylor. And yet ever since the dawn of the Renaissance had subsisted a conflict between reason and faith. From the first, indeed, the Christian religion had affirmed the existence of such a conflict, and had even based its plea upon its own weakness in it. In face of the classical culture, with its deep wide-struck roots in the world as it permanently exists, St. Paul asserted the claims of that which could not appeal with success to any genuinely human principle. Paradox as it was, that was the strength of the new spirit; for how much

is there at all times in humanity which cannot
appeal with success for encouragement or tol-
erance to any genuinely human principle. In
the Middle Ages it might seem that faith had
reconciled itself to philosophy; the Catholic
church was the leader of the world's life as well
as of the spirit's. Looking closer we see that
the conflict is still latent there; the supremacy
of faith is only a part of the worship of sorrow
and weakness which marks the age. The weak
are no longer merely a majority, they are all
Europe. It is not that faith has become one
with reason; but a strange winter, a strange
suspension of life, has passed over the classical
culture which is only the human reason in its
most trenchant form. Glimpse after glimpse,
as that pagan culture awoke to life the conflict
was felt once more. It is at the court of Fred-
erick II. that the Renaissance first becomes dis-
cernible as an actual power in European society. How definite and unmistakable is the
attitude of faith towards that! Ever since the
Reformation all phases of theology had been

imperfect philosophies, reluctant philosophies
—that is, in which there was a religious *arrière*
pensée; philosophies which could never be in
the ascendant in a sincerely scientific sphere.
The two elements had never really mixed.
Writers so different as Locke and Taylor have
each his liberal philosophy and each has his
defence of the orthodox belief; but, also, each
has a divided mind: we wonder how the two
elements could have existed side by side;
brought together in a single mind, but unable
to fuse in it, they reveal their radical con-
trariety. The Catholic church and humanity
are two powers that divide the intellect and
spirit of man. On the Catholic side is faith,
rigidly logical as Ultramontanism, with a proportion of the facts of life, that is, all that is
despairing in life coming naturally under its
formula. On the side of humanity is all that
is desirable in the world, all that is sympathetic
with its laws, and succeeds through that sympathy. Doubtless, for the individual, there are
a thousand intermediate shades of opinion, a

thousand resting-places for the religious spirit; still, τὸ διορίζειν οὐκ ἔστι τῶν πολλῶν, fine distinctions are not for the majority; and this makes time eventually a dogmatist, working out the opposition in its most trenchant form, and fixing the horns of the dilemma; until, in the present day, we have on one side Pius IX., the true descendant of the fisherman, issuing the Encyclical, pleading the old promise against the world with a special kind of justice; and on the other side, the irresistible modern culture, which, as religious men often remind us, is only Christian accidentally.

The peculiar temper of Coleridge's intellect made the idea of reconciling this conflict very seductive. With a true speculative talent he united a false kind of subtlety and the full share of vanity. A dexterous intellectual *tour de force* has always an independent charm; and therefore it is well for the cause of truth that the directness, sincerity, and naturalness of things are beyond a certain limit sacrificed in vain to a factitious interest. A method so

forced as that of Coleridge's religious philosophy is from the first doomed to be insipid, so
soon as the temporary interest or taste or curiosity it was designed to meet has passed away.
Then, as to the manner of such books as the
Aids to Reflection, or *The Friend:*—These
books came from one whose vocation was
in the world of art; and yet, perhaps, of all
books that have been influential in modern
times, they are farthest from the classical form
—bundles of notes—the original matter in-
separably mixed up with that borrowed from
others—the whole just that mere preparation
for an artistic effect which the finished artist
would be careful one day to destroy.   Here,
again, we have a trait profoundly characteristic
of Coleridge.   He often attempts to reduce a
phase of thought subtle and exquisite to conditions too rough for it.   He uses a purely
speculative gift in direct moral edification.
Scientific truth is something fugitive, relative,
full of fine gradations; he tries to fix it in absolute formulas.   The *Aids to Reflection,* or

The Friend, is an effort to propagate the
volatile spirit of conversation into the less
ethereal fabric of a written book; and it is only
here and there that the poorer matter becomes
vibrant, is really lifted by the spirit.

At forty-two, we find Coleridge saying, in a
letter: —

"I feel with an intensity unfathomable by words
my utter nothingness, impotence, and worthlessness
in and for myself. I have learned what a sin is
against an infinite, imperishable being such as is the
soul of man. The consolations, at least the sensible
sweetness of hope, I do not possess. On the con-
trary, the temptation which I have constantly to
fight up against is a fear that, if annihilation and the
possibility of heaven were offered to my choice, I
should choose the former."[1]

What was the cause of this change? That is
precisely the point on which, after all the gossip
there has been, we are still ignorant. At times
Coleridge's opium excesses were great; but
what led to those excesses must not be left out
of account. From boyhood he had a tendency

[1] Quoted in Gillman's *Life of Coleridge.*

to low fever, betrayed by his constant appetite
for bathing and swimming, which he indulged
even when a physician had opposed it.   In
1803, he went to Malta as secretary to the English Governor.   His daughter suspects that the
source of the evil was there, that for one of his
constitution the climate of Malta was deadly.
At all events, when he returned, the charm of
those five wonderful years had failed at the
source.

De Quincey said of him, "he wanted better
bread than can be made with wheat."   Lamb
said of him that from boyhood he had "hun-
gered for eternity."   Henceforth those are the
two notes of his life.   From this time we must
look for no more true literary talent in him.
His style becomes greyer and greyer, his
thoughts *outré,* exaggerated, a kind of cre-
dulity or superstition exercised upon abstract
words.   Like Clifford, in Hawthorne's beautiful romance—the born Epicurean, who by
some strange wrong has passed the best of his
days in a prison—he is the victim of a division

of the will, often showing itself in trivial things: he could never choose on which side of the garden path he would walk. In 1803, he wrote a poem on *The Pains of Sleep.* That unrest increased. Mr. Gillman tells us "he had long been greatly afflicted with nightmare, and when residing with us was frequently aroused from this painful sleep by any one of the family who might hear him."

That faintness and continual dissolution had its own consumptive refinements, and even brought as to the *Beautiful Soul,* in *Wilhelm Meister,* a faint religious ecstasy—that singing in the sails which is not of the breeze. Here, again, is a note of Coleridge's:—

"In looking at objects of nature while I am thinking, as at yonder moon, dim-glimmering through the window-pane, I seem rather to be seeking, as it were asking, a symbolical language for something within me that already and for ever exists, than observing anything new. Even when that latter is the case, yet still I have always an obscure feeling, as if that new phenomenon were the dim awakening of a forgotten or hidden truth of my inner nature." Then, "while

I was preparing the pen to write this remark, I lost the train of thought which had led me to it."

What a distemper of the eye of the mind! What an almost bodily distemper there is in that!

Coleridge's intellectual sorrows were many; but he had one singular intellectual happiness. With an inborn-taste for transcendental philosophy, he lived just at the time when that philosophy took an immense spring in Germany, and connected itself with a brilliant literary movement. He had the luck to light upon it in its freshness, and introduce it to his countrymen. What an opportunity for one reared on the colourless English philosophies, but who feels an irresistible attraction towards metaphysical synthesis! How rare are such occasions of intellectual contentment! This transcendental philosophy, chiefly as systematized by Schelling, Coleridge applies with an eager, unwearied subtlety to questions of theology.

.   .   .   .

The vagueness and fluidity of Coleridge's theological opinions have been exaggerated through an illusion, which has arisen from the occasional form in which they have reached us. Criticism, then, has to methodize and focus them. They may be arranged under three heads: the general principles of supernaturalism, orthodox dogmas, the interpretation of Scripture. With regard to the first and second, Coleridge ranks as a Conservative thinker; but his principles of Scriptural interpretation resemble Lessing's; they entitle him to be regarded as the founder of the modern liberal school of English theology. By supernaturalism is meant the theory of a divine person in immediate communication with the human mind, dealing with it out of that order of nature which includes man's body and his ordinary trains of thought, according to fixed laws, which the theologian sums up in the doctrines of "grace" and "sin." Of this supernaturalism, the *Aids to Reflection* attempts to give a metaphysical proof. The first necessity of

the argument is to prove that religion, with its
supposed experiences of grace and sin, and the
realities of a world above the world of sense, is
the fulfilment of the constitution of every man,
or, in the language of the "philosophy of nature," is part of the "idea" of man; so that
when those experiences are absent all the rest
of his nature is unexplained, like some enig-
matical fragment, the construction and working of which we cannot surmise. According to
Schelling's principle, the explanation of every
phase of life is to be sought in that next above
it. This axiom is applied to three supposed
stages of man's reflective life: Prudence,
Morality, Religion. Prudence, by which Coleridge means something like Bentham's "en-
lightened principle of self-preservation," is, he
says, an inexplicable instinct, a blind motion in
the dark, until it is expanded into morality.
Morality, again, is but a groundless prepposses-
sion until transformed into a religious recognition of a spiritual world, until, as Coleridge
says in his rich figurative language, "like the

main feeder into some majestic lake, rich with hidden springs of its own, it flows into and becomes one with the spiritual life." A spiritual life, then, being the fulfilment of human nature, implied, if we see clearly, in those instincts which enable one to live on from day to day, is part of the "idea" of man.

The second necessity of the argument is to prove that "the idea," according to the principle of the "philosophy of nature," is an infallible index of the actual condition of the world without us. Here Coleridge introduces an analogy:

"In the world, we see everywhere evidences of a unity, which the component parts are so far from explaining, that they necessarily presuppose it as the cause and condition of their existing as those parts, or even of their existing at all. This antecedent unity, or cause and principle of each union, it has, since the time of Bacon and Kepler, been customary to call a law. This crocus for instance; or any other flower the reader may have before his sight, or choose to bring before his fancy; that the root, stem, leaves, petals, &c., cohere to one plant is owing to an antecedent power or principle in the seed which existed before a single particle of the matters that constitute the size and visibility of the crocus had been attracted from the surrounding soil, air, and moisture.   Shall we turn to the seed? there, too, the same necessity meets us: an antecedent unity must here, too, be supposed.   Analyse the seeds with the finest tools, and let the solar microscope come in aid of your senses, what do you find?—means and instruments; a wondrous fairy tale of nature, magazines of food, stores of various sorts, pipes, spiracles, defences; a house of many chambers, and the owner and inhabitant invisible."—*Aids to Reflection.*

Nature, that is, works by what we may call intact ideas.   It coordinates every part of the crocus to all the other parts; one stage of its growth to the whole process; and having framed its organism to assimilate certain external elements, it does not cheat it of those elements, soil, air, moisture.   Well, if the "idea" of man is to be intact, he must be enveloped in a supernatural world; and nature always works by intact ideas.   The spiritual life is the highest development of the idea of man; there must be a supernatural world corresponding to it.

One finds, it is hard to say how many, difficulties in drawing Coleridge's conclusion. To
mention only one of them—the argument looks
too like the exploded doctrine of final causes.
Of course the crocus would not live unless the
conditions of its life were supplied. The flower
is made for soil, air, moisture, and it has them;
just as man's senses are made for a sensible
world, and we have a sensible world. But give
the flower the power of dreaming, nourish it on
its own reveries, put man's wild hunger of
heart and susceptibility to *ennui* in it, and what
indication of the laws of the world without it
would be afforded by its longing to break its
bonds?

In theology people are content with anal-
ogies, probabilities, with the empty schemes of
arguments for which the data are still lacking;
arguments, the rejection of which Coleridge
tells us implies "an evil heart of unbelief," but
of which we might as truly say that they derive
all their consistency from the peculiar atmosphere of the mind which receives them. Such

arguments are received in theology because
what chains men to a religion is not its claim on
their reason, their hopes or fears, but the glow
it affords to the world, its *beau ideal.* Coleridge thinks that if we reject the supernatural,
the spiritual element in life will evaporate also,
that we shall have to accept a life with narrow
horizons, without disinterestedness, harshly cut
off from the springs of life in the past. But
what is this spiritual element? It is the passion
for inward perfection with its sorrows, its
aspirations, its joy. These mental states are
the delicacies of the higher morality of the few,
of Augustine, of the author of the "Imitation,"
of Francis de Sales; in their essence they are
only the permanent characteristics of the
higher life. Augustine, or the author of the
Imitation, agreeably to the culture of their
age, had expressed them in the terms of a metaphysical theory, and expanded them into what
theologians call the doctrines of grace and sin,
the fluctuations of the union of the soul with
its unseen friend. The life of those who are

capable of a passion for perfection still pro-
duces the same mental states; but that religious
expression of them is no longer congruous with
the culture of the age. Still, all inward life
works itself out in a few simple forms, and culture cannot go very far before the religious
graces reappear in it in a subtilised intellectual
shape. There are aspects of the religious character which have an artistic worth distinct from
their religious import. Longing, a chastened
temper, spiritual joy, are precious states of
mind, not because they are part of man's duty
or because God has commanded them, still less
because they are means of obtaining a reward,
but because like culture itself they are remote,
refined, intense, existing only by the triumph of
a few over a dead world of routine in which
there is no lifting of the soul at all. If there is
no other world, art in its own interest must
cherish such characteristics as beautiful spec-
tacles. Stephen's face, "like the face of an
angel," has a worth of its own, even if the
opened heaven is but a dream.

Our culture, then, is not supreme, our intellectual life is incomplete, we fail of the intellectual throne, if we have no inward longing,
inward chastening, inward joy. Religious belief, the craving for objects of belief, may be refined out of our hearts, but they must leave
their sacred perfume, their spiritual sweetness,
behind. This law of the highest intellectual life
has sometimes seemed hard to understand.
Those who maintain the claims of the older and
narrower forms of religious life against the
claims of culture are often embarrassed at finding the intellectual life heated through with the
very graces to which they would sacrifice it.
How often in the higher class of theological
writings—writings which really spring from
an original religious genius, such as those of
Dr. Newman—does the modern aspirant to
perfect culture seem to find the expression of
the inmost delicacies of his own life, the same
yet different! The spiritualities of the Christian life have often drawn men on little by little
into the broader spiritualities of systems op-

posed to it—pantheism, or positivism, or a philosophy of indifference. Many in our own generation, through religion, have become dead to religion. How often do we have to look for some feature of the ancient religious life, not in a modern saint, but in a modern artist or philosopher! For those who have passed out of Christianity, perhaps its most precious souvenir is the ideal of a transcendental disinterestedness. Where shall we look for this ideal? In Spinoza; or perhaps in Bentham or in Austin.

Some of those who have wished to save supernaturalism—as, for instance, Theodore Parker—have rejected more or less entirely the dogmas of the Church. Coleridge's instinct is truer than theirs; the two classes of principles are logically connected. It was in defence of the dogmas of the Church that Coleridge elaborated his unhappy crotchet of the diversity of the reason from the understanding. The weakness of these dogmas had ever been not so much a failure of the authority of Scripture or tradition in their favour, as their conflict with reason that they were words rather than conceptions. That analysis of words and conceptions which in modern philosophy has been a principle of continual rejuvenescence with Descartes and Berkeley, as well as with Bacon and Locke, had desolated the field of scholastic theology. It is the rationality of the dogmas of that theology that Coleridge had a taste for proving.

Of course they conflicted with the understanding, with the common daylight of the mind, but then might there not be some mental faculty higher than the understanding? The history of philosophy supplied many authorities for this opinion. Then, according to the "philosophy of nature," science and art are both grounded upon the "ideas" of genius, which are a kind of intuition, which are their own evidence. Again, this philosophy was always saying the ideas of the mind must be true, must correspond to reality; and what an aid to faith is that, if one is not too nice in distinguishing between ideas and mere convictions, or prejudices, or habitual views, or safe opinions! Kant also had made a distinction between the reason and the understanding. True, this harsh division of mental faculties is exactly what is most sterile in Kant, the essential tendency of the German school of thought being to show that the mind always acts *en masse*. Kant had defined two senses of reason as opposed to the understanding. First, there was the "speculative reason," with its "three categories of totality," God, the soul, and the universe—three mental forms which might give a sort of unity to science, but to which no actual intuition corresponded. The tendency of this part of Kant's critique is to destroy the rational groundwork of theism. Then there was the "practical reason," on the relation of which to the "speculative," we may listen to Heinrich Heine:—

"After the tragedy comes the farce. (The tragedy is Kant's destructive criticism of the speculative reason.) So far, Immanuel Kant has been playing the

relentless philosopher; he has laid siege to heaven."
Heine goes on with some violence to describe the havoc
Kant has made of the orthodox belief—"Old Lampe,[1]
with the umbrella under his arm, stands looking on
much disturbed, perspiration and tears of sorrow
running down his cheeks. Then Immanuel Kant
grows pitiful, and shows that he is not only a great
philosopher but also a good man. He considers a
little; and then, half in good nature, half in irony,
he says, 'Old Lampe must have a god, otherwise the
poor man will not be happy; but man ought to be
happy in this life, the practical reason says that;
let the practical reason stand surety for the existence of a god; it is all the same to me.' Following
this argument, Kant distinguishes between the theoretical and the practical reason, and, with the
practical reason for a magic wand, he brings to life
the dead body of deism, which the theoretical reason
had slain."

Coleridge first confused the speculative reason with the practical, and then exaggerated
the variety and the sphere of their combined
functions. Then he has given no consistent
definition of the reason. It is "the power of
universal and necessary convictions;" it is "the

[1] The servant who attended Kant in his walks.

knowledge of the laws of the whole considered as one;" it is "the science of all as a whole." Again, the understanding is "the faculty judging according to sense," or "the faculty of means to mediate ends;" and so on. The conception floating in his mind seems to have been a really valuable one; that, namely, of a distinction between an organ of adequate and an organ of inadequate ideas. But when we find him casting about for a definition, not precisely determining the functions of the reason, making long preparations for the "deduction" of the faculty as in the third volume of *The Friend*, but never actually starting, we suspect that the reason is a discovery in psychology which Coleridge has a good will to make, and that is all; that he has got no farther than the old vague desire to escape from the limitations of thought by some extraordinary mystical faculty. Some of the clergy eagerly welcomed the supposed discovery. In their difficulties they had often appealed in the old simple way to sentiment and emotion as of a higher authority than the understanding, and on the whole had had to get on with very little philosophy.   Like M. Jourdain, they were amazed to find that they had been all the time appealing to the reason; now they might actually go out to meet the enemy.   Orthodoxy might be cured by a hair of the dog that had bitten it.

Theology is a great house, scored all over with hieroglyphics by perished hands. When we decipher one of those hieroglyphics, we find in it the statement of a mistaken opinion; but knowledge has crept onward since the hand dropped from the wall; we no longer entertain the opinion, and we can trace the origin of the mistake.   Dogmas are precious as memorials of a class of sincere and beautiful spirits, who in a past age of humanity struggled with many tears, if not for true knowledge, yet for a noble and elevated happiness.   That struggle is the substance, the dogma only its shadowy expression; received traditionally in an altered age, it is the shadow of a shadow, a mere τρίτον εἴδωλον, twice removed from substance and reality. The true method then in the treatment of dogmatic theology must be historical. Englishmen are gradually finding out how much that method has done since the beginning of modern criticism by the hands of such writers as Baur. Coleridge had many of the elements of this method: learning, inwardness, a subtle psychology, a dramatic power of sympathy with modes of thought other than his own. Often in carrying out his own method he gives the true historical origin of a dogma, but with a strange dulness of the historical sense, he regards this as a reason for the existence of the dogma now, not merely as reason for its having existed in the past. Those historical elements he could not envisage in the historical method, because this method is only one of the applications, the most fruitful of them all, of the relative spirit.

After Coleridge's death, seven letters of his on the inspiration of Scripture were published, under the title of *Confessions of an Inquiring*

Spirit. This little book has done more than any other of Coleridge's writings to discredit his name with the orthodox. The frequent occurrence in it of the word "bibliolatry," borrowed from Lessing, would sufficiently account for this pious hatred. From bibliolatry Coleridge was saved by the spiritualism, which, in questions less simple than that of the infallibility of Scripture, was so retarding to his culture. Bibliolators may remember that one who committed a kind of intellectual suicide by catching at any appearance of a fixed and absolute authority, never dreamed of resting on the authority of a book. His Schellingistic notion of the possibility of absolute knowledge, of knowing God, of a light within every man which might discover to him the doctrines of Christianity, tended to depreciate historical testimony, perhaps historical realism altogether. Scripture is a legitimate sphere for the understanding. He says, indeed, that there is more in the Bible that "finds" him than he has experienced in all other books put together. But

still, "There is a Light higher than all, even
the Word that was in the beginning. If between this Word and the written letter I shall
anywhere seem to myself to find a discrepance,
I will not conclude that such there actually is;
nor on the other hand will I fall under the con-
demnation of them that would lie for God, but
seek as I may, be thankful for what I have—
and wait." Coleridge is the inaugurator of
that *via media* of Scriptural criticism which
makes much of saving the word "inspiration,"
while it attenuates its meaning; which supposes a sort of modified inspiration residing in
the whole, not in the several parts. "The
Scriptures were not dictated by an infallible
intelligence;" nor "the writers each and all
divinely informed as well as inspired." "They
refer to other documents, and in all points express themselves as sober-minded and vera-
cious writers under ordinary circumstances are
known to do." To make the Bible itself "the
subject of a special article of faith, is an unne-
cessary and useless abstraction."

His judgment on the popular view of inspiration is severe. It is borrowed from the
Cabalists; it "petrifies at once the whole body
of Holy Writ, with all its harmonies and sym-
metrical gradations;—turns it at once into a
colossal Memnon's head, a hollow passage for a
voice, a voice that mocks the voices of many
men, and speaks in their names, and yet is but
one voice and the same;—and no man uttered it
and never in a human heart was it conceived."
He presses very hard on the tricks of the "rou-
tiniers of desk and pulpit;" forced and fantastic interpretations; "the strange—in all
other writings unexampled—practice of bringing together into logical dependency detached
sentences from books composed at the distance
of centuries, nay, sometimes a millennium,
from each other, under different dispensations,
and for different objects."

Certainly he is much farther from bibliolatry
than from the perfect freedom of the humanist
interpreters. Still he has not freed himself
from the notion of a sacred canon; he cannot

regard the books of Scripture simply as fruits of the human spirit; his criticism is not entirely disinterested. The difficulties he finds are chiefly the supposed immoralities of Scripture; just those difficulties which fade away before the modern or relative spirit, which in the moral world as in the physical traces everywhere change, growth, development. Of historical difficulties, of those deeper moral difficulties which arise for instance from a consideration of the constitutional unveracity of the Oriental mind, he has no suspicion. He thinks that no book of the New Testament was composed so late as A. D. 120.

Coleridge's undeveloped opinions would be hardly worth stating except for the warning they afford against retarding compromises. In reading these letters one never doubts what Coleridge tells us of himself: "that he loved truth with an indescribable awe," or, as he beautifully says, "that he would creep towards the light, even if the light had made its way through a rent in the wall of the temple." And yet there is something sad in reading them by the light which twenty-five years have thrown back upon them.   Taken as a whole, they contain a fallacy which a very ardent lover of truth might have detected.

The Bible is not to judge the spirit, but the spirit the Bible.   The Bible is to be treated as a literary product.   Well, but that is a conditional, not an absolute principle—that is not, if we regard it sincerely, a delivery of judgment, but only a suspension of it.   If we are true to the spirit of that, we must wait patiently the complete result of modern criticism.   Coleridge states that the authority of Scripture is on its trial—that at present it is not known to be an absolute resting-place; and then, instead of leaving that to aid in the formation of a fearless spirit, the spirit which, for instance, would accept the results of M. Renan's investigations, he turns it into a false security by anticipating the judgment of an undeveloped criticism. Twenty-five years of that criticism have gone by, and have hardly verified the anticipation.

WORDSWORTH

THE appearance of Prof. Knight's judicious *Selections,* and of Messrs. Macmillan's collected edition of his works in one volume, with the first book of *The Recluse,* now printed in its entirety for the first time, and a sensible introductory essay by Mr. John Morley, gives sufficient proof that general interest in Wordsworth is on the increase. Nothing could be better—nothing so well calculated as a careful study of Wordsworth to correct the faults of our bustling age as regards both thought and taste, and remind people, amid the vast contemporary expansion of the means and accessories of life, of the essential value of life itself.

The Complete Poetical Works of William Wordsworth. With an introduction by John Morley.

The Recluse.

Selections from Wordsworth. By William Knight and other Members of the Wordsworth Society. With Preface and Notes.

It was none other than Mill himself, so true a
representative of the main tendencies of the
spirit of our day, who protested that when the
battle which he and his friends were waging
had been won the world would "need more
than ever those qualities which Wordsworth
had kept alive and nourished."

In the new edition the poems are arranged,
with their dates, as much as possible in the
order of their composition—an arrangement
which has its obvious uses for the student of the
development of the poet's genius, though the
older method of distributing his work into various groups of subject had its service as throwing light upon his poetic motives, more especially as coming from himself.

Mr. Morley in his introduction dwells on the
fact of Wordsworth's singular personal happiness as having had much to do with the physiognomy of his work—a calm, sabbatic, mystic
well-being some may think it; worldly pros-
perity De Quincey reckoned it. The poet's
own flawless temperament, his fine mountain

atmosphere of mind, had, of course, something
to do with that. What a store of good fortune,
what a contribution to happiness in the very
finest sense of that word, is really involved in
a cheerful, grateful, physical temperament,
above all for a poet!

An intimate consciousness of the expression
of natural things, which weighs, listens, penetrates, where the earlier phase of mind passed
roughly by, is a large element in the complexion of modern poetry. It has been re-
marked as a fact in mental history again and
again. It reveals itself in many forms, but is
certainly strongest and most attractive in the
most characteristic products of modern literature as of modern art also: it is exemplified
almost equally by writers as unlike each other
as Senancour and Théophile Gautier. As a
curious chapter in the history of human mind,
its growth might be traced from Rousseau to
Chateaubriand, from Chateaubriand to Victor
Hugo. It has doubtless some latent connexion with those pantheistic theories which

locate an intelligent soul in material things, and have largely exercised men's minds in some modern systems of philosophy; while it makes as much difference between ancient and modern landscape art as there is between the rough masks of an early mosaic and a portrait by Reynolds or Gainsborough. Of this new sense the writings of Wordsworth are the central and elementary expression; he is more simply and entirely preoccupied with it than any other poet, though there are fine expressions of precisely the same interest in so different a poet as Shelley. There was in Wordsworth's own character, as we have seen, a certain natural contentment, a sort of inborn religious placidity, seldom found united with a sensibility so mobile as his, which was favourable to the quiet, habitual observation of inanimate or imperfectly animate existence His life of eighty years is divided by no very profoundly felt incidents, its changes being almost wholly inward; it falls, like his work, into broad, untroubled, perhaps somewhat monotonous spaces. What it resembles most is the life of one of those early Flemish or Italian painters who, just because their minds were full of heavenly visions, passed, some of them, the better part of sixty years in quiet systematic industry. And this sort of placid life matured in Wordsworth a quiet unusual sensibility, really innate in him, to the sights and sounds of the natural world. It is to this world, and to a world of congruous meditation thereon, that we see him retiring in this newly published poem of *The Recluse*—taking leave, without much count of costs, of the world of business, of action and ambition, as also of all that, for the majority of mankind, counts as sensuous enjoyment.

And so it came about that this sense of a life, a living soul, in natural objects, which in most poetry is but a rhetorical artifice, is with Wordsworth the assertion of what for him is almost literal fact. To him every natural object seemed to possess more or less of a moral or spiritual life—to be capable of a companionship with humanity full of expression, of inex-

plicable affinities, and delicacies of intercourse.
It was like a survival, in the peculiar intellectual temperament of a man of letters at the end
of the eighteenth century, of that primitive
condition which some philosophers have traced
in the general history of human culture, in
which all outward objects alike, including even
the works of men's hands, were believed to be
endowed with animation, and the world seemed
"full of souls." The eighteenth century had
had but little of such mysticism. But then
Wordsworth was essentially a leader of the revolt against the hard reign of the mere understanding in that century, a pioneer of thoughts
which have been so different in our own.

And it was through nature thus ennobled
by a semblance of passion and thought that
Wordsworth approached the spectacle of human life. Human life, indeed, is for him at
first only an additional accidental grace upon
this expressive landscape. When he thought
of men and women, it was of men and women
as in the presence, and under the influence of

the spell, of those effective natural objects, and linked to them by many associations. The close connexion of humanity with natural objects, the habitual association of his feelings and thoughts with a particular neighbourhood —colourless perhaps, certainly limited—has sometimes seemed to degrade those who have been the subjects of its influence, as if it did but reinforce that physical connexion of our nature with the actual lime and clay of the soil which is always drawing us nearer to our end. But for Wordsworth these influences tended to the dignity of human nature, because they tended to tranquillise it. He raises nature to the level of human thought to give it power and expression; he subdues man to the level of nature, and gives him thereby a certain breadth and vastness and solemnity. The "leech-gatherer" on the moor, the "woman stepping westward," are for him natural objects, almost in the same sense as the aged thorn or the lich-ened rock on the heath. In this sense the leader of the "Lake School," in spite of an earnest preoccupation with man, his thoughts, his destiny, is the poet of nature.

And of nature, after all, in its modesty. The English lake country has, of course, its grandeurs. But the peculiar function of Wordsworth's genius, as carrying in it a power to open out the soul of apparently little or familiar things, would have found its true test had he become the poet of Surrey, say, and the prophet of its life. The glories of Italy and Switzerland, though he did write a little about them, had too potent a material life of their own to serve greatly his poetic purpose.

In Wordsworth's prefatory advertisement to the first edition of *The Prelude,* published in 1850, it is stated that that work was intended to be introductory to *The Recluse,* and that *The Recluse,* if completed, would have consisted of three parts. The second part is *The Excursion.* The third part was only planned; but the first book of the first part was left in manuscript by Wordsworth—though in manuscript, it is said, in no great condition of

forwardness for the printers. This book, now
for the first time printed *in extenso* (a very
noble passage from it found place in that prose
advertisement to *The Excursion*), is the
great novelty of this latest edition of Wordsworth's poetry: it was well worth adding to
the poet's great bequest to English literature.
A true student of his work, who has formulated
for himself what he supposes to be the leading
characteristics of Wordsworth's genius, will
feel, we think, lively interest in testing them by
the various fine passages in what is here pre-
sented for the first time. Let the following
serve for a sample:—

Thickets full of songsters, and the voice
Of lordly birds, an unexpected sound
Heard now and then from morn to latest eve,
Admonishing the man who walks below
Of solitude and silence in the sky?
These have we, and a thousand nooks of earth
Have also these, but nowhere else is found,
Nowhere (or is it fancy?) can be found
The one sensation that is here; 'tis here,
Here as it found its way into my heart

In childhood, here as it abides by day,
By night, here only; or in chosen minds,
That take it with them hence, where 'er they go.
—'Tis, but I cannot name it, 'tis the sense
Of majesty, and beauty, and repose,
A blended holiness of earth and sky,
Something that makes this individual spot,
This small abiding-place of many men,
A termination, and a last retreat,
A center, come from wheresoe'er you will,
A whole without dependence or defect,
Made for itself, and happy in itself,
Perfect contentment, Unity entire.

A NOVEL BY MR. OSCAR WILDE

("THE PICTURE OF DORIAN GRAY.")

THERE is always something of an excellent talker about the writing of Mr. Oscar Wilde; and in his hands, as happens so rarely with those who practise it, the form of dialogue is justified by its being really alive. His genial, laughter-loving sense of life and its enjoyable intercourse, goes far to obviate any crudity there may be in the paradox, with which, as with the bright and shining truth which often underlies it, Mr. Wilde, startling his "countrymen," carries on, more perhaps than any other writer, the brilliant critical work of Matthew Arnold. *The Decay of Lying,* for instance, is all but unique in its half-humorous, yet wholly convinced, presentment of certain valuable truths of criticism. Conversational ease, the fluidity of life, felicitous expression, are qual-

ities which have a natural alliance to the suc-
cessful writing of fiction; and side by side with
Mr. Wilde's *Intentions* (so he entitles his critical efforts) comes a novel, certainly original,
and affording the reader a fair opportunity of
comparing his practise as a creative artist with
many a precept he has enounced as critic concerning it.

A wholesome dislike of the common-place,
rightly or wrongly identified by him with the
bourgeois, with our middle-class—its habits
and tastes—leads him to protest emphatically
against so-called "realism" in art; life, as he
argues, with much plausibility, as a matter of
fact, when it is really awake, following art—
the fashion an effective artist sets; while art,
on the other hand, influential and effective art,
has never taken its cue from actual life.   In
Dorian Gray he is true certainly, on the whole,
to the æsthetic philosophy of his *Intentions;*
yet not infallibly, even on this point: there is
a certain amount of the intrusion of real life
and its sordid aspects—the low theatre, the

pleasures and griefs, the faces of some very unrefined people, managed, of course, cleverly enough. The interlude of Jim Vane, his half-sullen but wholly faithful care for his sister's honour, is as good as perhaps anything of the kind, marked by a homely but real pathos, sufficiently proving a versatility in the writer's talent, which should make his books popular. Clever always, this book, however, seems to set forth anything but a homely philosophy of life for the middle-class—a kind of dainty Epicurean theory, rather—yet fails, to some degree, in this; and one can see why. A true Epicureanism aims at a complete though harmonious development of man's entire organism. To lose the moral sense therefore, for instance, the sense of sin and righteousness, as Mr. Wilde's heroes are bent on doing as speedily, as completely as they can, is to lose, or lower, organisation, to become less complex, to pass from a higher to a lower degree of development. As a story, however, a partly supernatural story, it is first-rate in artistic management; those Epicurean niceties only adding to the decorative colour of its central figure, like so many exotic flowers, like the charming scenery and the perpetual, epigrammatic, surprising, yet so natural, conversations, like an atmosphere all about it. All that pleasant accessory detail, taken straight from culture, the intellectual and social interests, the conventionalities, of the moment, have, in fact, after all, the effect of the better sort of realism, throwing into relief the adroitly-devised supernatural element after the manner of Poe, but with a grace he never reached, which supersedes that earlier didactic purpose, and makes the quite sufficing interest of an excellent story.

We like the hero, and in spite of his somewhat unsociable devotion to his art, Hallward, better than Lord Henry Wotton. He has too much of a not very really refined world in and about him, and his somewhat cynical opinions, which seem sometimes to be those of the writer, who may, however, have intended Lord

Henry as a satiric sketch. Mr. Wilde can
hardly have intended him, with his cynic amity
of mind and temper, any more than the miserable end of Dorian himself, to figure the motive
and tendency of a true Cyrenaic or Epicurean
doctrine of life. In contrast with Hallward,
the artist, whose sensibilities idealise the world
around him, the personality of Dorian Gray,
above all, into something magnificent and
strange, we might say that Lord Henry, and
even more the, from the first, suicidal hero,
loses too much in life to be a true Epicurean—
loses so much in the way of impressions, of
pleasant memories, and subsequent hopes,
which Hallward, by a really Epicurean econ-
omy, manages to secure. It should be said
however, in fairness, that the writer is imper-
sonal: seems not to have identified himself entirely with any one of his characters: and
Wotton's cynicism, or whatever it may be, at
least makes a very clever story possible. He
becomes the spoiler of the fair young man,
whose bodily form remains un-aged; while his

picture, the *chef d'oeuvre* of the artist Hallward, changes miraculously with the gradual
corruption of his soul. How true, what a light
on the artistic nature, is the following on actual
personalities and their revealing influence in
art. We quote it as an example of Mr. Wilde's
more serious style.

"I sometimes think that there are only two eras of
any importance in the world's history. The first is
the appearance of a new medium for art, and the
second is the appearance of new personality for art
also. What the invention of oil-painting was to the
Venetians, the face of Antinous was to late Greek
sculpture, and the face of Dorian Gray will some
day be to me. It is not merely that I paint from
him, draw from him, sketch from him. Of course
I have done all that. But he is much more to me
than a model or a sitter. I won't tell you that I
am dissatisfied with what I have done of him, or that
his beauty is such that art cannot express it. There
is nothing that art cannot express, and I know that
the work I have done, since I met Dorian Gray, is
good work, is the best work of my life. But in some
curious way his personality has suggested to me an
entirely new manner in art, an entirely new mode of
style. I see things differently, I think of them

differently. I can now recreate life in a way that was hidden from me before."

Dorian himself, though certainly a quite unsuccessful experiment in Epicureanism, in life as a fine art, is (till his inward spoiling takes visible effect suddenly, and in a moment, at the end of his story) a beautiful creation. But his story is also a vivid, though carefully considered, exposure of the corruption of a soul, with a very plain moral, pushed home, to the effect that vice and crime make people coarse and ugly. General readers, nevertheless, will probably care less for this moral, less for the fine, varied, largely appreciative culture of the writer, in evidence from page to page, than for the story itself, with its adroitly managed supernatural incidents, its almost equally wonderful applications of natural science; impossible, surely, in fact, but plausible enough in fiction. Its interest turns on that very old theme, old because based on some inherent experience or fancy of the human brain, of a double life: of Döppelgänger—not of two *persons,* in this case, but of the man and his portrait; the latter of which, as we hinted above, changes, decays, is spoiled, while the former, through a long course of corruption, remains, to the outward eye, unchanged, still in all the beauty of a seemingly immaculate youth —"the devil's bargain." But it would be a pity to spoil the reader's enjoyment by further detail. We need only emphasise, once more, the skill, the real subtlety of art, the ease and fluidity withal of one telling a story by word of mouth, with which the consciousness of the supernatural is introduced into, and maintained amid, the elaborately conventional, sophisticated, disabused world Mr. Wilde depicts so cleverly, so mercilessly. The special fascination of the piece is, of course, just there —at that point of contrast. Mr. Wilde's work may fairly claim to go with that of Edgar Poe, and with some good French work of the same kind, done, probably, in more or less conscious imitation of it.

A POET WITH SOMETHING TO SAY

THE student of modern literature, turning to the spectacle of our modern life, notes there a variety and complexity which seem to defy the limitations of verse structure, as if more and more any large record of humanity must necessarily be in prose. Yet there is certainly abundant proof that the beauty and sorrow of the world can still kindle satisfying verse, in a volume recently published under the significant title of *Nights and Days* being, in effect, concentrations, powerful, dramatic, of what we call the light and shadow of life; although, with art, as Mr. Symons conceives:—

> Since, of man with trouble born to death
> She sings, her song is less of Days than Nights.

Readers of contemporary verse who may regret in much of it, amid an admirable achievement of poetic form, a certain lack of poetic matter, will find substance here—abundant poetic substance, developing as by its own organic force, the poetic forms proper to it, with natural vigours.

Mr. Symons's themes then, are almost exclusively those of the present day, studied, as must needs happen with a very young writer, rather through literature than life; through the literature, however, which is most in touch with the actual life around us. *"J'aime passionnément la passion,"* he might say with Stendhal: and in two main forms. The reader of Dante will remember those words of La Pia in the *Purgatorio,* so dramatic in their brevity that they have seemed to interpret many a problematic scene in pictorial art. Shape their exacter meaning as we may, they record an instance of human passion, under the influence of some intellectual subtlety in the air, going to its end by paths round-about. Love's casuistries, impassioned satiety, love's inversion into cruelty, are experiences even more characteristic of our late day than of

Dante's somewhat sophisticated middle age; and it is just this complexion of sentiment— a grand passion entangled in scruples, refinements, after-thoughts, reserved, repressed, but none the less masterful for that, conserving all its energies for expression in some unexpected way—that Mr. Symons presents, with unmistakable insight, in one group of his poems, at the head of which he should place *An Act of Mercy*—odd and remote, mercy's self turned malignant—or *A Revenge,* or, perhaps in long-drawn sonnet-series, *A Lover's Progress*—progress one-half at least, in merely intellectual fineness, as if love had heard *All the Yea and Nay of Life,* and taken his degree in some school of metaphysical philosophy. Like the hero in his own *Interlude of Helena and Faustus,* the modern lover, as Mr. Symons conceives him, claims to have seen in their fulness

The workings of the world Plato but dreamt of.

He welcomes, as an added source of interest

in the study of it, the curious subtlety to which the human soul has come even in its passions.

"Thy speech hath not the largeness of my sires," says Helena to Faustus; but this "largeness" Mr. Symons attains in just the converse of this remotely conceived, exotic, casuistical passion, in that rural tragedy, the tragedy of the poor generally (the tyranny of love, here too, sometimes turning to cruelty) in a group of poignant stories, told with unflinching dramatic sincerity, which is not afraid of the smallest incident that has the suggestion of true feeling in it. The elementary passions of men and women in their exclusive strength, the fierce, vengeful sense of outraged honour in the humble, wild hunger, in mortal conflict with the ideal of homely dignity, as Crabbe or Wordsworth understood it, and beyond these miserable ragged ends of existence, the white dawn possible for humanity, for *Esther Bray,* for *Red Bredbury,* for *Margery of the Fens* whose wronged honour and affection has made her a witch:

"Go and leave me alone.   I'm past your help, I shall
    lie,
As she lay, through the night, and at morn, as she
    went in the rain, I shall die.
Go and leave me alone.   Let me die as I lived.   But
    oh,
If the wind wouldn't cry and wail with the baby's
    cry as I go!"

And this too, the tragedy of the poor as it
must always be with us, finds its still more
harshly satiric in verse in certain poems, like
A Café Singer and other Parisian gro-
tesques, for the delineation of the deepest
tragedy of all, underlying that world of sickly
gaslight and artificial flowers which apes the
tuberose conventionalities of the ultra-refined;
often with a touch of lunacy about it, or the
partial lunacy of narcotism—"the soul at
pawn"—or that violent religious reaction which
is like a narcotic.   These very modern notes
also are made to contribute their gloom to the
dramatic effect of life in these poems.

Set over against this impressively painted
series of nights and days, often forbidding, a

faith in the eternal value of art is throughout maintained;

"Art alone
Changeless among the changing made;"

as amply compensating for all other defects in the poet is finding of things; though on what grounds we hardly see, except his own deep, unaffected sense of it. Its witness to eternal beauty comes in directly, as nature itself, with tranquillising influence, contrives to do in this volume, in interludes of wholesome air, as through open doors, upon those hot, impassioned scenes. Yet close as art comes in these very poems, for example, to the lives of men, to interpret the beauty and sorrow there, Mr. Symons is anxious to disavow any practical pretension to alter or affect the nature of things thereby:

"She probes an ancient wound yet brings no balm."

And yet pity (who that reads can doubt it?) is a large constituent of this writer o' temper—natural pity contending with the somewhat

artificial modern preference for telling and
having a story in all its harsh unrelieved effect.
The appeal of a pale, smitten face has perhaps
never been rendered more touchingly than in
A Village Mariana.

The complex, perhaps too matterful, soul of
our century has found in Mr. Browning and
some other excellent modern English poets,
the capacity for dealing masterfully with it, ex-
cepting only that it has been too much for their
perfect lucidity of mind, or at least of style, so
that they take a good deal of time to read. In
an age of excellent poets, people sometimes
speculate wherein any new and original force
in poetry may be thought likely to reveal itself;
and some may have thought that just as, for
a poet after Dryden, nothing was left but correctness, and thereupon the genius of Pope became correct, with a correctness which made
him profoundly original; so the *cachet* of a
new-born poetry for ourselves may lie precisely
in that gift of lucidity, given a genuine grapple
with difficult matter. The finer pieces in this

volume, certainly, any poet of our day might be glad to own, for their substance, their dramatic hold on life, their fine scholarship; and they have this eminent merit among many fine qualities of style—readers need fear no difficulty in them. In this new poet the rich poetic vintage of our time has run clear at last.

MR. GEORGE MOORE AS AN ART CRITIC

("MODERN PAINTING.")

THE writer of this clever book deserves to be heard about his opinions on fine art; and especially on the somewhat vexed subject of *Modern Painting*. He deserves to be heard because he has a right to those opinions, having taken more pains than critics of contemporary art sometimes do to know from within what he is writing about; while he writes with all the courage of the opinions thus sincerely formed, so as to keep the attention of the reader fixed to the very last page. If those qualities make him a pungent critic of what he disapproves of what he may think mistaken general tendencies in art, or of particular works in which this or that artist seems to fall below his own proper level, they make him also—those qualities of

142

painstaking, of conviction and liveliness—a very animating guide to the things he loves, and in particular to the modern painting of France, of which we in England still know so little, though a large number of us desire to know more.

With all his French intuitiveness and *Gaillardise* Mr. Moore is a patient teacher, knows what and how to explain to those who are "without" and explains clearly. The persons or professional bodies of persons whom he attacks would, of course, have a reply; and the more permanently true, certainly, the more delightful parts of his volume, at all events for the sincere lover of art, are his chapters of positive appreciation concerning the French masters of his choice—Ingres, Degas, Millet and others. Mr. Moore, at least so far as French art is concerned, is Catholic in his taste.

Mr. Moore makes so pleasant a guide to French art partly because he is in full sympathy with France—French scenery, the French character. Now the genius of Ingres is cosmopolitan like that of those old Greek artists with whom Mr. Moore fearlessly ranks him. But Mr. Moore does not love cosmopolitanism in art; he thinks, perhaps rightly, that art is in its very nature a matter of personal or, in its larger groupings, of national, inspiration. To be cosmopolitan, he tells us, to be one and the same at all times and places, is the somewhat doubtful privilege of science. He might urge, perhaps, in the presence of the works of Ingres, that the French are the Greeks of our contemporary world, and that with both alike a certain "cosmopolitanism" was, in truth, an element of "national" character. But then Ingres is also certainly academic in a high degree; and Mr. Moore has no love for academies, at least in art, in regard to which territory he holds that to be something of a gypsy (it is his own figure), to have no law and no responsibilities except to one's own native preference, is the veritable citizenship. And yet Mr. Moore really has the secret of Ingres, of that somewhat abstract academic, cosmopolitan and uncoloured painting of which *La Source* is the best known example.

"Think of the learning and the love that were necessary for the accomplishment of such exquisite simplifications. Never did pencil follow an outline with such penetrating and unwearying passion, or clasp and enfold it with such simple and sufficient modelling. Nowhere can you detect a starting point or a measurement taken; it seems to have grown as a beautiful tendril grows, and every curve sways as mysteriously, and the perfection seems as divine. Beside it Dürer would seem crabbed and puzzle-headed; Holbein would seem angular and geometrical; Da Vinci would seem vague; and I hope that no critic by partial quotation will endeavour to prove me guilty of having said that Ingres was a greater artist than Da Vinci. I have not said any such thing; I have merely striven by aid of comparison to bring before the reader some sense of the miraculous beauty of one of Ingres's finest pencil drawings."

That is said of one of Ingres's pencil drawings in the Louvre, a study for the *Odalisque*. How different, how unmistakably different, alike in germ and development, was the genius of Corot! Mr. Moore with no effect of incongruity, treats of them, side by side, in a single chapter. Corot, the elusive and evanescent master of Barbizon, whose work he also values duly, loves better probably than that of the very definite and half-classic Ingres, is, however, far more difficult to write about. He is ingeniously compared with Rembrandt.

"They painted with the values—that is to say with what remains on the palette when abstraction has been made of the colouring matter—a delicate neutral tint of infinite subtlety and charm; and it is with this, the evanescent and impalpable soul of the vanished colours, that the most beautiful pictures are painted. Corot, too, is a conspicuous example of this mode of painting. His right to stand among the world's colourists has never, so far as I know, been seriously contested; his pictures are almost void of colouring matter—a blending of grey and green, and yet the result is of a richly coloured evening."

Corot and Rembrandt indeed arrived at the same goal by similar methods.

"Rembrandt told all that a golden ray falling through a darkened room awakens in a visionary brain; Corot told all that the grey light of morning and evening whispers in the pensive mind of the elegiac poet. The story told was widely different, but the manner of telling was the same. One attenuated in the light, the other attenuated in the shadow. Both sacrificed the corners with a view to fixing the attention on the one spot in which the soul of the picture lives."

The reader may now judge fairly of Mr. Moore's manner of writing; may think there is something in it of the manner of the artists he writes of. It is perhaps a surprise, yet certainly of a pleasant sort, to find one who is so hard in his characterisation of what may be not urgently called "vulgar errors" in matters of art, so reverent and delicate when he comes to treat of things delicate. He seems to be really in possession of their "secret," as of Sisley also and Chavannes, of Manet and of Monet, who with sparkling magic—or trick—paints "in a series of little dots." He is "the only painter to whom the word "impressionism" may be reasonably applied.

"Not with half-tints in which colour disappears

are Monet and his school concerned, but with the
brilliant vibration of colour in the full light, with
open spaces where the light is reflected back and
forward, and nature is but a prism filled with
dazzling and iridescent tints."

There is much besides in this volume of considerable interest but of which there is hardly
space to speak here. In common, these chapters have certainly this merit, that, by their
very conviction, their preferred conviction, they
arouse the general reader, lost probably in a
general sleep of conventional ideas, at the very
least to combat so incisive a visitor—put up his
back perhaps by a claim for unfamiliar views;
challenge him to come honestly to convictions
for himself, different enough, it may be, from
Mr. Moore's.

A lover of French art, in its various phases,
the drift of Mr. Moore's charge against contemporary English art, especially under academic patronage, is that it is not vernacular;
that the degenerate sons of Reynolds and
Constable are leaving their native earth, and

with it the roots and sources of their own proper strength, actually for this very France of his own preference. Impressionism, to use that word, in the absence of any fitter one—the impressionism which makes his own writing on art in this volume so effective—is, in short, the secret of both his likes and dislikes, his hatred of what he thinks conventional and mechanic, together with his very alert and careful evaluation of what comes home to him as straightforward, whether in Reynolds or Rubens, or Ruysdael, in Japan, in Paris or in modern England; with Mr. Whistler for instance and Mr. Sargent; his belief in the personal, the uncontrollable. Above all that can be learnt in art, he would assure us—beyond all that can be had of teachers—there is something there, something in every veritable work of art, of the incommunicable, of what is unique, and this is perhaps the one thing really of value in art. As a personal quality or power it will vary greatly in the case of this or that work or workman, in its appeal to those who, being outsiders in the matter of art, are nevertheless sensitive and sincerely receptive towards it. It will vary also, in a lesser degree, even to those who in this matter *really know*. But to the latter, at all events, preference in art will be nothing less than conviction and the estimate of artistic power and product, in every several case, an object of no manner of doubt at all, such as may well give a man, as in Mr. Moore's own case, the courage of his opinions. In such matter opinion is, in fact, of the nature of the sensations one cannot help.

WALTER PATER.

Hum
PN
761
P3
1969

DATE DUE

DEC 29 1970

MAR 15 1971

MAR 15 1974

NOV 15 1990